Don't say 'G'day' to the Queen
Broadcasts from Thatcher's Britain

Paula Lucas

Illustrated by Paula Lucas and Rob Julian

Copyright © 2009 by Paula Lucas
Additional illustrations copyright © 2009 by Rob Julian

The majority of the items included in this volume have been broadcast on BBC Radio 4 under the name Jean Foster.

The right of Paula Lucas to be identified as the Author of the work has been asserted by her in accordance with the Copyright, Designs and Patents Act 1988.

Apart from any use permitted under UK copyright law, this publication may only be reproduced, stored, or transmitted, in any form, or by any means, with prior permission in writing of the publishers, or, in the case of reprographic production, in accordance with the terms of the licenses issued by the Copyright Licensing Agency.

First published in 2009 by Siligalah Press
Wymondham, Norfolk, UK

siligalah.press@btinternet.com

ISBN 978-0-9564292-0-9

Don't say 'G'day' to the Queen
Broadcasts from Thatcher's Britain

For Dad and the Kids
Who all turned out better than expected

Contents

Don't say G'day to the Queen	9
I was a teenage heart case	15
All for my own good	20
Camping	23
The music goes round and round	27
The lonely goatherd	31
Good news is no news	35
Maternity for beginners	39
Cows in the night	43
Afloat at home and abroad	47
Agents	52
Butchers' rights	56
On being a good citizen	60
Education	64
Of class and classics	68
The joys of little children	72

Hats	76
Hair	80
God rest ye merry, gentlepersons	84
Fishing for Milton Keynes	87
Dunnies	91
Christmas down under	94
Words and phrases	98
Weather	103
Saturday night at the movies	107
Jet trails in the sunset	111
Mayday, mayday	117
Busy doing nothing	121
Noztalgia	126
Notes	129

DON'T SAY 'G'DAY' TO THE QUEEN

Welcome to the fascinating subject of Me. I'm forced to discourse upon myself because I am the only subject I know anything about; and so it was on this subject, particularly with reference to my experience of being an immigrant from the antipodes, that I occasionally spoke on BBC Radio 4's *Woman's Hour* more than twenty years ago.

I emigrated with my husband and two small children from Adelaide, South Australia, in 1980, when my husband was offered a professorship at London University.

Before we left, several academic friends offered us advice on how to survive the culture shock of English society, though in most cases it was more an attempt to limit the danger of *me* shocking *it*, Alpha Male's[1] colleagues anticipating his rocketing to stardom and being precipitated into polite society. When I told a somewhat literal Oxford grad that, in the event of us ever being invited to the palace, I would make a point of wearing my hat with corks around it, she recoiled in horror.

'Heavens, no, you mustn't do that!' She exclaimed. 'It would be too awful!' She didn't actually add 'And for goodness sake don't say G'day to the Queen!' but I could see the words hovering about her lips.

---

[1] Hereinafter referred to as Al, or A.M. in the peculiarly irritating style of Victorian writers, but mostly as 'my husband'.

I thought this was a bit rich from someone who had fallen for an Australian PhD student and ended up in the Colonies.

As it happened A.M.'s colleagues were correct in their assumptions and he was called on to meet Her Maj and other members of the clan a few times, but on each occasion I was either uninvited or safely in the background. I have quailed – as who does not – before the indomitable Princess Royal (though my quailing was as nothing compared to that of the poor blighter who had to introduce us) and I did once commit the faux pas of saying 'How do you do' to Princess Alexandra – a gaffe, I was informed *sotto voce* by a cringing fellow-guest as the Princess smiled charmingly and moved on, almost as bad as saying 'G'day'.

I have to confess that when I finally did get to the Palace – an investiture – not mine, as you'll no doubt have guessed – I didn't wear a hat with dangling corks. Mainly because I don't have one. I wore a fantastic black straw and feather creation worthy of one of my Edwardian predecessors, which cost an immense amount of money and which I have never worn since because the brim is so wide I can't see where I'm going in it, but which I can't bear to part with.

Well, enough of the Royals. Now back to me.

I enrolled in a local WEA class in creative writing, and the tutor suggested I submit one of my assignments, a personal anecdote about my mother's attempts at matchmaking, to *Woman's Hour,* as she thought it might be suitable short filler between longer items.

So I duly posted off a neatly typed script to BBC Broadcasting House, Portland Place, London, and absolutely nothing happened. Not even a bland acknowledgement of its arrival. After a while I stopped eagerly scanning the post and assumed that my effort had been deemed unworthy and binned – particularly since another member of the class had had a swift and positive response to a script she'd submitted to Radio 4's fifteen minute programme *Morning Story*, and her story, read by a professional actor, was broadcast not long afterwards.

So it was a complete surprise when a year later, I was telephoned by someone from *Woman's Hour* who said that they would like to broadcast my piece, and would I like to come in and record it myself? And she explained apologetically that the long silence was due to the script having fallen behind a filing cabinet on arrival, having only just been discovered, presumably during a spring clean. ('I'm so pleased that you have a *nice* Australian voice,' she said. 'I was really hoping you would have.' The implication being that if I had had a *nasty* Australian voice they would have had to use an actor. Or find another filing cabinet).

Naturally I was thrilled to the marrow, and quite prepared to overlook the fact that I had been scraped from the bottom of the furniture; and an appointment was made for me to go up and do the recording. I fronted up at the Portland Place building with its legendary Eric Gill sculpture above the entrance – the one of Prospero and naked Ariel, the size of whose penis Lord Reith allegedly ordered the sculptor to reduce in the interests of public decency – and was whisked up several floors and introduced to producer Kay Evans, who took me into a small dark room containing a couple of chairs on either side of a desk on which stood one of those old-fashioned microphones more usually seen in photographs of wartime monarchs giving a Christmas Speech. We sat opposite one another, and Kay asked me what I had had for breakfast, for sound level. I think I said 'Nothing, I was too nervous,' and she said 'Just make something up' and I said 'Porridge, sausages and scrambled egg' or something and she said 'That's fine' and instructed me to read my anecdote, which I did. And then she took me somewhere – I suppose it must have been the BBC canteen – for a drink and a sandwich, and I had a whisky and soda to celebrate and soaked myself in soda-water, never having used a soda-siphon before, and went to sleep on the tube going home. Or maybe that was on another occasion, because as a result of that first piece I was asked to do a few more, and from October 1982 to some time in 1985 I recorded 28 three- to five-minute-long scripts that were used, along with contributions from other writers, to fill in awkward gaps between interviews and serious features.

The first broadcast went out under my own name, but when I discovered that it had been heard by an Australian acquaintance visiting London who happened by chance to have the car radio on, I felt I should go incognito to spare my family's blushes and adopted the pseudonym Jean Foster. Whenever I was due to be broadcast I'd be telephoned by the BBC shortly beforehand, and I managed to record most of my pieces for posterity using a cassette recorder next to the radio. I sent a selection of these back to my parents and brothers in Adelaide – my father was a radio technician and was naturally chuffed that a family member had made it as an Artist, even in such a lowly capacity, at the hallowed BBC. Eventually I even sent them my first effort, the one about my matchmaking mother, hoping that she would realise that it was intended as an affectionate portrait and not be hurt. I never found out; but she did continue to speak to me.

After the first, the recordings were read in well-lit studios with flashing monitors and glass screens behind which grumpy sound engineers told me off for rustling my script. I hadn't realised how much skill is involved in soundlessly discarding one piece of paper and taking up another and it was something I never mastered. In the end I had to type my scripts in single-spaced tiny print so that I could get the lot onto one piece of paper.

I wrote about anything that took my fancy – shopping, clothes, child-rearing, Christmas, homesickness, the weather – the nearest I came to controversy was when I got a bit hot under the collar about alleged Animal Rights groups breaking butcher-shop windows.

I did once get to participate in a live broadcast, when in about 1983 during a particularly bad bushfire season in Australia I was interviewed briefly by Sue MacGregor and read part of a letter my father had sent about fires around Adelaide. On that occasion I even got to eat Maureen Lipmann's sandwiches. Not sandwiches made *by* Maureen Lipmann, you understand, but *for* her, in her capacity of chief interviewee for the day. She declined – probably one of the reasons she remains svelte and I don't – and the studio crew and I ate them instead.

As I worked very slowly with lots of crossings-out and rewriting, it used to take me three or four days to produce a script lasting a few minutes, so we would certainly have starved if I'd been the sole breadwinner.

I was given an 'Artist Number' and was paid for each contribution – £8 for my very first piece in 1982. That was exactly the price of a rather cute crescent-moon shaped night light with a smiley man-in-the moon face in a shop I passed on my way to Wimbledon station to go up to the BBC. I was very tempted to buy it in order to be able to say that I had bought the moon with my creative earnings, but in the end I didn't. Just over two years later I was paid £60 for an item. I like to think that at that point *Woman's Hour* decided I had become too high maintenance, rather than the more likely truth that I had become boring and tedious, when they gave me the 'Don't call us, we'll call you' treatment. They haven't called since, and after 20-odd years it seems a bit unlikely they will. So not exactly J K Rowling, then, but it was fun while it lasted.

And since these little anecdotes have been gathering mould like fine Stilton for some time, I've taken the liberty of giving them another airing, with a bit of minor editing, and the inclusion of a couple that weren't aired at the time. I've kept the punctuation to preserve the rhythm of the spoken word. Keep in mind that at the time they were broadcast there were no mobile phones or Wiis,

Global Warming was just a cloud on the horizon and there were Smoking sections on aircraft. And I was 35 and better looking than I thought.

I WAS A TEENAGE HEART CASE

I was born with a hole in my heart. At least that's what the doctor told my mother, though she confided to me recently that she'd always suspected that there was nothing wrong with me, and it was all a conspiracy by surgeons anxious to practice a new technique. My aunt told me after the operation that I'd had *two* holes, but she was a known embroiderer of medical histories.

Whatever the truth was, at the age of fifteen I was patched up with a piece of polystyrene[1] and afterwards led a life of remarkable dullness.

Until then life had been pretty interesting, the most interesting thing in it being me. I was a professional hypochondriac at three. I just loved hospitals – the perfume of polish and ether, the hush and rush, the gleaming tools. Most of all I loved the cavernous Out-Patients waiting room at the Adelaide Children's Hospital, with it's frieze of Australian Marsupials – the cuscus was my favourite – and the ladies in the Red Cross canteen who sold sticky buns, and tea in glass cups.

Little actual discomfort was involved. My few opportunities to practice Noble Suffering occurred when I had blood taken, and I was able to watch with practised indifference a succession of perspiring technicians desperately searching for a non-collapsible vein.

---

[1] Or something. I'm not a surgeon.

It was fun being an object of medical interest. It had all the rewards of acting without the labour. I simply exposed my chest and looked cute, and was given admiration and jelly beans. Amiable doctors let me borrow their stethoscopes and called me 'Tiger'. There was no treatment. I was simply measured, prodded, and X-rayed while the experts talked over my head of new surgical techniques being used in America and the possibility of their future use in Australia. Then they'd show me my X-rays, pat me on the head and send me home glowing with satisfaction. So I rather enjoyed my disability. That is, until I started school.

Until then I had communicated almost exclusively with adults, and the sight of fifty strangers my own size made me recoil in dismay. Having had so much practice at Noble Suffering I didn't *cry* when my mother left like some of the others, but my superiority was brief. I was a year older than most, knew no games, and couldn't tie my own shoelaces. Unlike the other children I hadn't been to kindergarten to learn these essentials. Nevertheless, I might have fitted in if the curriculum hadn't been so *physical*.

I didn't *look* handicapped. As well as being the oldest in the class I was also the tallest. Except in cold weather, when my lips turned an interesting shade of blue, I looked the picture of health. I was instantly branded a malingerer, and it was generally felt that what I needed most was exercise.

Protest was useless. Over the years I learnt to go along with the farce – netball, hurdling, running round the oval – to the point of collapse, when I would be dismissed contemptuously as a liability to the team and allowed to spend sports period doing my homework, until next year. From time to time my mother wrote notes requesting that I be excused games, but they were considered forgeries. In Grade 4, I was enlisted to race on sports day. Possessing neither shorts nor plimsolls[1] I ran in full uniform – including lace-up shoes – the endless asphalt track. On leaden feet I staggered in last to the stifled sniggers of the school, and collapsed in tears. A motherly infant teacher completed my humiliation by clasping me to her bosom and giving me sixpence 'for trying'.

It was a relief when we moved to the country, where sport was taken seriously, and I was allowed to act as scorekeeper and equipment carrier.

At twelve I had my first operation.

Open-heart surgery was well established in Australia by then, and already several little boys had been flown in from Papua New Guinea (where congenital heart defects seem to have been particularly common) for surgery. They appeared in the newspapers in 'Before' and 'After' photos, frail and appealing or cheekily grinning, and declared their ambitions to become star footballers when the stitches came out. There were also one or two girls, of a devastating frailty and charm, who intended making careers in ballet.

I debated with myself whether, when my turn came, to go for ballet too or admit that my ambition was to become a librarian.

My schoolmates anticipated reflected glory. They may also have experienced a pleasurable *frisson* at the possibility that I might not survive the anaesthetic. When it happened that all I could show afterwards was a small scar inside my right elbow and not even a line in the local press, their scorn was withering. This had been merely a preamble, a cardiac catheterisation to determine the site of the leakage. Despite my vivid description of the experience of having a tube pushed through a vein *and right inside my heart* while *conscious* and surrounded by cathode-ray tubes, they were unimpressed.

---

[1] We called them sandshoes.

By the time the real thing came around, three years later (by which time I was in high school and had failed to master ballroom dancing or any form of gymnastics) nobody was remotely interested. The operation had become almost routine and was no longer news, even when performed on adorable toddlers. Even my mother spent most of the visiting hour adjusting her make-up in the reflective surface of the metal plate that surrounded the oxygen mask connection by the bed.

Eventually I was carted away to theatre and put to sleep. But not before I'd had time to observe a heart-lung machine the size of a small garden shed, through which my blood was to be diverted, next to the operating table. During the next eight hours I was partly frozen, had my ribs broken, and any holes (if they existed) patched. I awoke in an oxygen tent, feeling as if I had been trampled by a rogue elephant and somehow been left to expire in the Arctic Circle, wearing only a loincloth and a few bandages.

After defrosting I was moved, bruised and aching, to the surgical ward. On my locker stood an ominous black box with a dial.

Two wires from it disappeared through my bandaged ribs.

I was seized by an almost overwhelming urge to turn the dial, just to see what would happen. The thought gave me palpitations, and for the first time I was aware of the actual possibility of Death, and lay rigid and sleepless lest I inadvertently rip out my connections and cause my instant demise. When the pacemaker and I were officially parted a day or two later I was enormously relieved.

Three weeks later I was discharged, with a slight, fashionable Murmur, a huge scar across my chest, and the assurance that I was now normal. I could have ballet lessons, climb mountains, have babies or even (my scar being horizontal and not vertical) wear a bikini.

For years I took up none of these options, being too tall, too frightened, or too fat. At last, feeling that I ought

I was a teenage heart case 19

to justify my existence after everybody's trouble, I had a couple of babies.

On reflection, I think I should have taken up ballet.

ALL FOR MY OWN GOOD

When I was approaching nineteen my mother decided that it was time she introduced me to some men. It was obvious that I wasn't going to do anything and if something didn't happen soon I might never get married. Marriage was still mandatory for women in Australia in 1965, divorce not yet being fashionable. In any case, marriage was a prerequisite for divorce, as well as the two-point five children, triple-fronted cream brick bungalow and family car.

I was terrified of men at nineteen. As a matter of fact I was pretty scared of women. At thirty-six, I'm only really twitchy with children. I might make a reasonably well-adjusted grandmother. But back in 1965, Mum decided that desperate action was needed, and she knew that it would have to be devious, because any hint of her true intentions would blow the whole plan, the object of which was to place me, and a man, in close enough proximity for him to ask me out. She felt sure that once cornered, I would be too spineless to refuse.

She went to a Matrimonial Agency run by one Elizabeth Hay, whose name was well known to anyone who read the Misc. column of the *Adelaide Advertiser* classifieds, and who probably would have been outraged at the suggestion that she ran a Lonely Hearts Club. She'd been in business so long she was practically a pillar of society.

She agreed to send along any number of young men willing to comply with my mother's deception.

A couple were 'the sons of old army friends' Mum 'just happened to meet in town', who dropped in to say hullo. One she claimed to have met on a bus. He was 'a recent arrival in the city', without friends or family, and she'd taken pity on his loneliness and invited him to tea. There were similar fictions, the details of which I've forgotten.

I only know that, out of the blue, always when Dad was working a late shift and my brothers had been sent to bed early, these strange young men began to arrive in the evenings, all looking sort of eager and apprehensive at the same time.

Mum would insist on me dressing up, because it was bad manners to sit around in sloppy old skirts and jumpers when visitors were coming; what would they think? She'd spend half the day spring-cleaning the house and then, when the visitor arrived, she'd introduce us and say 'Well, I'll just go and make a cup of tea,' and disappear for several hours.

The young man and I would engage in self-conscious small talk for a while and then he'd bring the conversation round to films, and ask me out to the pictures.

The first time it happened I was so surprised I actually laughed. He looked so hurt and cross I apologised immediately and said yes, of course, I'd love to go to *The Sound of Music* with him; it just seemed rather sudden.

The preliminary battle having been won, my mother would then appear with the tea.

My suspicions crystallised when a prematurely bald, twenty-something teacher from the High School I'd graduated from the year before, turned up. (He made his excuses and left). Yet the idea seemed so utterly fantastic – surely even *my* mother would not do anything quite so outrageous – that I rejected it, at first.

I finally discovered the facts when one of the prospective suitors, who somehow hadn't been fully briefed, wrote to me. His letter began

'Dear Paula, I got your name from…'

The following line had been heavily scored out in dark blue ink and the name 'Bob Jones' (one of the earlier suitors) written in above it. 'You sound like a nice girl' it went on 'and I think we might have things in common…' This was *too* much. I soaked the page in a saucer of water until enough of the ink had cleared away to enable me to see the name 'Elizabeth Hay' and confronted my mother. (It was a measure of her desperation that, having intercepted the letter in the first place, rather than destroying it she risked discovery in an effort to add yet another male to my string).

'I did it all for your own good!' she said.

And in a way she had, because, inspired by righteous indignation, I packed my bags and went to Darwin to be a nurse.

It was a few years before I was actually married. I thought Mum would be overjoyed. But as I was about to leave for the Church, she gave me a funny sort of look and said 'Well dear, I hope you're doing the right thing.'

She gave my veil a straightening tweak. 'Never mind,' she added briskly ' If you don't like it, you can always get a divorce.'

CAMPING

Whenever I mention camping, I hear the sound of hollow laughter from my husband. It's odd, but he thinks I don't like camping. He seems to feel that any indication on my part of not relishing every little experience, right down to the flies drowning themselves in the billy tea, is proof that I'm not a camper at heart. Of course this is rubbish. I do enjoy camping. Especially afterwards when I'm looking at the slides. And the longer afterwards it is, the better I like it. After a few years I begin to get itchy feet, and start looking at tents and sleeping bags in catalogues. But whenever I mention the nifty little gadget I've discovered that simultaneously poaches eggs and washes socks over a campfire, he changes the subject.

I suspect that I'm destined never to have a camping holiday in Britain, unless I go by myself. Perhaps that is the answer. We could each get ourselves a rucksack and one of those little roll-up tents and go off to opposite ends of the country, with one child apiece. The following year, we could swap ends, and children. Then I could curse and weep on the nights when the tent refused to go up in the middle of a hailstorm, and sit huddled miserably over a smoking pile of wet sticks, reading the Bed and Breakfast Guide, without feeling that I was spoiling anyone's holiday.

And next morning I could rise to birdsong and marvel at the dawn sky, filling my nostrils with the scent of new-mown hay and woodsmoke, and start afresh, guilt-free. While he could sleep uncomplaining at the other end of the country in his sodden sleeping bag (in the unlikely event that he'd been silly enough to get it wet) and rise to birdsong, etc., without having his pleasure in the morning spoilt by a night spent in the company of a whingeing woman with a copy of the Bed and Breakfast Guide. I haven't mentioned the children's likely reactions because we've never taken them camping; but I think they could cope. After all, I've been whingeing, and their father's been strong and silent, since before they were born, so *our* behaviour would come as no surprise. And they'd only be stuck with me one year out of two.

Before I could put this scheme into practice, though, I'd need a stringent course in bodybuilding. I'm not at my best with a tent in a hailstorm. There are sure to be many women about who can raise a tent with the flick of a wrist, not to mention men who couldn't hammer a peg into the ground to save their lives. It just happens that, in *our* family, the man is the one with the muscles.

He also has the enormous advantage of not feeling the cold even in sub-arctic conditions, while I turn blue in a light breeze.

There are few experiences better calculated to turn a fun-loving fiancée into a wet blanket than having spent the night in one. That happened on our first camping trip. There we were, snugly zipped into our respective bedding, atop the newspapers that were supposed to keep out the cold from below, listening to the soporific drumming of rain on the canvas.

And as I lay there, feeling the ribs and elbows of Mother Earth digging into mine, I idly reached up and drew one finger along the canvas roof above my head. To this day I don't know *why* I did this, but believe me, I'll never do it again. Where my finger had touched, a long line of drips appeared, and fell upon me. All night.

It completely altered my attitude to the next day's planned activities. Unable to proffer the B. and B. Guide (hostelries being few and far between in the bush) I had to be content with going all miserable and monosyllabic.

When he pointed out that I should have known enough physics to realize what would happen if I touched the canvas, I'm afraid I said something uncharitable. Indeed our camping career might have ended right there, if it hadn't been for the University Field Trip.

Our party consisted of a botanist, two biologists and two biologist's wives, of whom I was one.

Water was scarce on this trip. We were rationed to half a cup a day each for ablutions. Much of the time soap-caked areas of my face seemed about to crack off, like old plaster. I could stand that. And the constant glitter of sun on the gibber, and the heat, the dust, and the flies. The problem was Bridge. The botanist, a fanatical devotee, had failed in his attempts to teach me the game.

He sat beside the campfire night after night in silent condemnation, playing a do-it-yourself game in a box. I think reluctant chivalry prevented him from asking the others to play, and making me a complete outcast.

But I could still be of some use as a driver. At least until the wheel fell off the trailer, somewhere North of Oodnadatta. Perhaps I *should* have noticed the rear-end wobble, but it was a rough road. And we *found* all the wheel bolts, even if it *did* mean a long walk back in the blazing sun.

And what if I didn't know the difference between Mulga and Wilga? Trees are trees. He was the botanist. When he said 'We'll camp at the next suitable clump of Wilga' I expected him to tell me when we'd arrived – not let me drive on for hours before asking 'Do you think you might find one you like before morning? We've been going through it for twenty miles.'

I swear, when I jabbed my sewing needle deep into his left calf it was an accident. At the time it seemed easier to mend the tear in his jeans with him still in them. We all make mistakes.

I'd really like to go away again, and pitch my tent by some murmuring stream, under the stars, and boil a billy on a neatly constructed campfire. It's such a pity nobody wants to go with me.

THE MUSIC GOES ROUND AND ROUND

Something I don't often admit is the fact that I can't really remember where I went on my honeymoon. That is, I remember that we did an awful lot of driving around the southern part of Australia, but individual towns merge in a sort of blur. This confession always produces knowing sniggers, and I mention it now only because of a song. There is one town I *do* remember clearly. It's Berri, on the river Murray, and I remember it because this song was playing on the car radio as we drove through.

Honey I think it was called – or possibly *Sunny* – anyway, it was an awful tearjerker full of mawkish male chauvinist sentiment, about this Honey (or Sunny) – the flower-like child-bride who died (the lyrics said 'She went away' but the real truth was obvious). There were many references to Angels, and Being Good, and the chorus, in which the singer said how much he missed her, made me cry.

I was dreadfully ashamed of this, so whenever it came up on the radio – which it frequently did – I stared fixedly out of the side window, holding my breath and clenching my fists between my knees, desperately hoping that my husband would not say something requiring an answer and make me betray myself. He never did. Perhaps the song had a similar effect on him, too, and he was too ashamed to admit it.

Well there I was, staring fixedly, and it was at the bulrushes swaying idly beside the river at Berri. We were driving along the road towards the ferry, rather slowly, perhaps (though this did not occur to me at the time) because his eyes were misty too, or perhaps merely in order to admire the view. The view is indelibly recorded on my mind; and it will always be associated with that song.

Just after we were married another song began to get a lot of airplay. It was *We've only just begun* by The Carpenters; all about white lace and promises and flying off into the rising sun, and it seemed peculiarly appropriate for us because not only were we newly married, but we had just flown off to America, where it seemed to be played all the time. Hearing it conjures up our apartment in Columbus, Ohio, from the open bedroom window of which I watched with delight my first real snowfall, unaware for some moments that I was being observed with shocked amazement by the tenant of the apartment opposite. I never found out whether he was shocked by my finding pleasure in the snow or the fact that I had no clothes on.

Pancakes with maple syrup for breakfast; walks in the park in the Fall, Halloween ghosts and goblins who wouldn't accept my homemade candy, Thanksgiving, Ground Hog Day – it all comes back with that song.

Then there's *Guantanamera* and *The Boy from Ipanema*, relics of an earlier past and first love: for a city named Darwin and a boy named Bob. Darwin is right at the top of Australia in the tropical Northern Territory; and I knew I loved it even before I saw it. I felt it, and smelled it. The plane from Adelaide landed after dark; and stepping out into the tropical night was like stepping into a bath full of warm tea. I know black velvet is more romantic, but tea was what I instantly thought of, sweet and dark and brown and scented with frangipani.

And when I looked up to the sky there were the faintly darker silhouettes of coconut palms. It was like something out of *South Pacific*. How could I resist?

Bob appeared in rather the same way. We met on a blind date arranged by a friend. Bob's effect on me was electric. To begin with he was in a romantic profession – the Royal Australian Air Force. The fact that he was a mechanic and not a pilot – the ultimate in Romance – only slightly dimmed his lustre. His hair was black and curly, his eyes were blue and his father was Irish.

We swam in the warm empty sea (it was not yet the tourist season) and the possibility of being stung by a Portuguese-man-o'war added a dash of danger. We walked long walks on pearly deserted beaches and sat beneath whispering palms watching poetic tropical sunsets.

But Bob was more interested in passion than poetry and when several tropical sunsets and all his inherited blarney failed (how narrowly he never knew) to gain his wicked ends he flew away.

At about the same time I discovered that I was not suited to follow in the footsteps of Florence Nightingale and resigned from nursing. For three weeks, while waiting for transport back to Adelaide, I lived alone in the house of an aunt who had gone to Brisbane, eating eggs scrambled with tinned pineapple (I was almost penniless and it was the only food she'd left behind) and walking by the sea suffering from a broken heart, which felt very much like indigestion. And for three weeks the local DJ played *Guantanamera* and *The Boy from Ipanema* on the radio. Play them again and it's all there – the pain, the palms, and the bedpans.

A couple of years ago I was delighted to hear, thumping in from the television where my children were watching Top of the Pops, the strains of *Green Door*, and then a nasal female wail announcing that it was her party and she'd cry if she wanted to.

The expression on the children's faces when I appeared flapping my tea towel in time to the music and singing along was one of disbelief.

'Do you *know* that song, Mum?'

'I knew it before you were born,' I replied. 'In fact I think *Grandma* probably knew it before *I* was born.'

'But it's on *Top of the Pops*!'

'I don't care,' I said, 'Uncle Geoffrey and I used to sing it when we were your age.'

They looked cheated. How dare they be served up *old* music, their expressions said?

I haven't really listened to pop music since the kids left school, so I don't know whether any other Golden Oldies have been revived lately.

But I hope they continue to throw the odd one in. They open up the past. Noel Coward was right. How potent cheap music is.

THE LONELY GOATHERD

Our first goat was a British Alpine named Misty. Actually, her full title was Misty Marshes the Second (or possibly Third) but we didn't use it. It seemed a bit pretentious for a goat whose sole purpose in life was to act as a lawn mower.

We bought her from a man who was selling off his herd of pedigreed milkers, and retiring. She would have been no use as a milker anyway, because she was sterile, but we weren't worried about that – what we were interested in was her capacity for large amounts of Salvation Jane,[1] a hairy and unpalatable weed, poisonous to other cattle, but eaten by goats with impunity. It has beautiful purple flowers that carpet the South Australian hills in spring, looking from a distance like a spread of bluebells, which just goes to show how deceptive a plant can be. In summer its dry woody stems, which rose to almost six feet over our septic tank, were a fire hazard on our ten acres of land. We thought that Misty could probably deal with a couple of acres in the paddock near the house.

Misty may have been sterile, but she was the epitome of femininity in both character and appearance. She was gentle, quiet, extremely well-bred, and beautiful to look at. Her horns were mere velvety bumps, though she did have a neat van Dyke beard. She had a glossy black and white coat and slim, elegant legs. She was certainly our most

---

[1] Viper's bugloss on Speed. Also known as Paterson's Curse.

impressive piece of livestock, which otherwise consisted of a couple of hives of bees and six free-range hens.

For a few days Misty fulfilled our highest expectations, eating everything in sight, including the bark on the Mallee trees shading her shelter shed. But quite suddenly she stopped eating anything at all, and moped listlessly by the gate, untempted even by oats. Although my husband had been raised on a dairy farm, he had no experience with goats, and I, a city girl, was completely ignorant. It had not occurred to us that Misty, snatched from the bosom of the herd, would pine.

But pine she did. It was obvious that unless we provided another goat fast, our lawn-mower would die of a broken heart.

When we had bought Misty there was a positive plethora of goats on the market. Now, there were none. We searched the livestock columns of the classified ads, we made local enquiries, but not a goat was to be had.

Misty was fading fast. Her thinness was becoming alarming, when at last a nanny goat was advertised in the local paper. There were no details and the price was suspiciously low, but I was not in a position to quibble. I telephoned, and bought her at once, and her owner obligingly drove her round in the back of his battered Volkswagen. He opened the passenger door and out clambered an animal with the sort of face that decorates the covers of paperbacks on Satanism.

Anne-Marie (as she was subsequently named) was a dirty white nanny with viciously curved horns and a nasty look in her pale yellow eyes. She also possessed a pendulous udder full of milk.

'I kept the kid,' her owner informed me. 'I only had her to keep the grass down, and there's not enough for two. She hasn't got a lot – milk her once a day and she'll soon dry off.'

So saying, he pocketed his money and left. Misty approached Anne-Marie with cautious interest. Anne-

Marie lowered her horns belligerently and gave a high-pitched snigger.

'Well, Misty,' I said, 'I've done my best. You'll just have to work things out between you.' And left them to it.

Some time later I heard the newcomer's ear-piercing bleating, and as the day wore on it grew more frequent, and more agonized. Reluctantly, knowing before I went what the trouble was, I investigated. She needed milking.

I had never milked a cow, let alone a goat, but I couldn't let the poor animal suffer. I'd had a similar experience myself with a refusenik newborn and I knew what she was going through – and by now it was late evening, and her udder was almost sweeping the ground.

The closest thing to a milk pail I had was an empty ice-cream carton. It seemed a pity to waste the milk, after all. I let myself into the paddock and approached the new possession gingerly.

'Come along then,' I murmured, soothingly. 'Milking time.' She rolled her eyes at me contemptuously and backed away. I clucked my tongue encouragingly and walked slowly forward. She backed off. I stood still. She stopped. I approached again. Again she backed away. I stopped, and examined the sky with feigned indifference. She stopped too.

'Come along now' I said. 'I'm not going to hurt you.'

'Mmmaaaaaaaaa!' she replied.

I stepped forward, she stepped back; and in this manner we proceeded around the paddock for about half an hour, watched with evident interest by Misty.

'Damn it all, Al's mother doesn't have this trouble with the cows.' I muttered. Then I remembered that the cows spent their milking time contentedly munching, so a bit of inducement might work on Anne-Marie as well. I fetched a container of oats and put it on the ground. Misty (whose interest in life was reviving by the minute) danced up and thrust her nose into it. Uttering an outraged bleat Anne-Marie galloped drunkenly forward and butted Misty aside with a swift jab of the horns, and proceeded to gobble.

When she seemed totally occupied I squatted down and put the ice-cream carton into position. She immediately put a hind foot in it. With a sigh, I reached out for her teats. At the first touch she leapt like a startled gazelle and cantered off to the opposite side of the paddock.

'Oh, suffer then, you dumb animal.' I hissed, and marched off in a huff. But within minutes her frustrated bleating was battering at my eardrums, and in desperation I telephoned my husband at work.

'Look,' I pleaded 'could you possibly come home early? I can't milk the goat.'

Half an hour later he was home. He opened the paddock gate and put the container of oats on the ground next to the gatepost. I was instructed to hold Misty by the collar, in case she should decide to bolt, though she was far too fascinated to bother.

When Anne-Marie lowered her head to the oats Al grabbed her collar, put a rope – the rope that had been hanging in our garage all the time – through it, tied her securely to the fence, and, using the gate as a crush to keep her backside still, milked her. To the great relief of all concerned.

'There.' He said. 'What's so difficult about that?'

'Nothing, I suppose' I admitted. 'It just never occurred to me to tie her up.'

He looked at me pityingly.

'Well it's a jolly good thing we didn't buy a farm,' he said.

Good news is no news

Ever since I can remember, and probably before that, the entire proceedings of the Australian Parliament have been broadcast on radio. Not merely the polite edited version, but the foot shufflings, bell-ringings and shouts of 'The Honourable Member for Wooloomooloo is a drongo, Mr. Speaker!'

Indeed the proceedings of Parliament are pure entertainment, but the most amusing speaker palls at 2 a.m., particularly on one's honeymoon. Well, to be strictly accurate, it was the week after the honeymoon, and we were freshly installed in our own little love-nest, when my husband switched on, as had been his wont when single, the late night session in Canberra and prepared to drift off to the Speaker's cries of 'Order! Order!' and 'The Ayes will pass to the right of the Chair, the Noes will pass to the left.' I cannot recall exactly how long I tolerated this intrusion into my domestic bliss, but there came a time when, baggy-eyed from lack of sleep, I issued the ultimatum.

'It's Parliament or me.' I said. 'There isn't room for all of us in this bed.'

I won.

Having succeeded in banishing the Lower House from my marriage-bed to Another Place I felt it prudent to concede the early-morning news. I should have pressed my advantage, but at the time I didn't realise the potential power of the young bride. Now that I do realise it I haven't got it any more, so I'm reduced to switching off the infernal machine the minute he gets into the shower. The clock-radio is a bedside fixture. The poor man is so addicted to disaster that he even takes the battery operated portable into the shower with him, turning up the volume so that he can hear the latest details above the roar of the water. When he goes away on conferences I switch over to radio three. What bliss it is to waken to the strains of *The Planet Suite* instead of *Star Wars*! But naturally, shortly after he arrives home again, it somehow gets shifted back.

He likes to wake up to radio 4. I like to wake up to radio 3, preferably after the news headlines. I have been known to concede, reluctantly, that news may be necessary, but at seven a.m. I feel that it is merely evil, and two hours of it, even with a five-minute break for *Thought for the Day*, positively excessive. Things are quite depressing enough without the added burden of learning, while struggling out of my early-morningmare, that while I slept 2000 people were wiped off the face of the earth by war, earthquake and disease, that my young are at risk from leaded petrol, radiation leaks, and drug pushers, and that even the gerbils are in imminent danger of liberation. Later in the day, after a certain amount of black coffee and a few mind-numbing household chores, I can usually face the facts with only moderate hysteria, and on rare occasions even watch the television news, where at least the physical characteristics of the newscasters provide a distraction.

I once heard a radio news editor say:
'Naturally we would like to be able to report that a family went to Brighton for a picnic, it was a lovely day, they all had a wonderful time, and nobody drowned, but unfortunately that's not news.' This dubious justification of his calling was in reply to a listener who, like myself, was feeling somewhat overburdened by the messages of global misery continually reinforced from *A.M.* to *A Book At Bedtime*.

It's all very well for my husband and his ilk, who have about twelve hours of Newslessness stretching endlessly between breakfast and tea, filled only by work. No wonder that, by nine p.m. they are positively gasping for a fix. Constant Listener and myself, on the other hand, are suffering from an overdose.

Radio 4 sustains us in our isolation both with fiction and the sort of facts we can live with comfortably. Things like the best way to prune roses, and how the oldest British female mountaineer coped with the fierce cold on Kanchenjunga; which apart from their intrinsic interest, give us something to talk about when the rest of the family comes in from the cold. But for Radio 4, we might actually forget how to speak.

Unfortunately it undoes most of the good thus achieved by repeatedly stuffing the World and National news down our earholes until we feel thoroughly crushed with guilt and misery, and just about ready to cut our own throats and those of any member of our family who actually arrives home from the jungle in one piece. Of course there may be others who react differently. Some people appear to view the news as a sort of endlessly fascinating fiction, like one of John Le Carre's novels, and they can't wait for the next instalment. Others may be so fired with indignation and inspiration that they desert fireside and family to join a medical corps in the Sudan or the guerrillas in Afghanistan.[1] I just want to curl up in a corner in the foetal position, whimpering.

Yes. I could simply turn it off. But by the time I've leapt across the room to hit the switch they've already hit me with the headlines. And turning off usually means forgetting to turn on again in time for *Woman's Hour*. Not reading the newspaper is much easier. I can manage that for days at a time.

Newspeople are fond of pointing out in their own defence that good news is no news – though exactly what is wrong with no news, no one has ever stated to my satisfaction – but this dictum does not apply in one area,

---

[1] In the early 1980's the Afghan mujahideen had Western support to fight a guerrilla war against the Soviet-backed regime.

and that is news about Royalty. Grim-faced television newscasters capable of relating the latest horrors in Beirut with finely judged solemnity suddenly come over all gooey at the merest glimpse of Princess This or Prince That doing anything, and the more trivial and domestic it is, the better. A sort of soppy, dewy-eyed-ness softens their forbidding features as they report the advent of Prince Harry's first tottering steps, or his Great-Grandmother's annual birthday wave, and as they drag their eyes away from the monitor it seems that they're just itching to reach out and give it an affectionate pat.

And long may it be so. Personally, I would be prepared to pay a special tax just to keep the Queen Mother in funny hats, if it would ensure her continued appearance in the news, along with the rest of her family. Long may they have slight colds, new dresses, be greeted by adoring crowds and have awnings collapse on their heads at official functions – they may be the only good news between me and divorce.

"It says 'The End is Nigh'"

MATERNITY FOR BEGINNERS

One of the many things that may happen to a woman when she becomes pregnant is the dissolution of the calcium from her bones and teeth into her bloodstream, leaving her with a permanent curvature of the spine, legs like jelly and teeth, if she has any left at all, that are grey and translucent, and have a tendency to crumble away on contact with anything stronger than custard. The theory is that this calcium is transferred to the growing baby, though just where it goes is mysterious, since the baby, upon delivery, also has legs like jelly and no teeth at all. But such are the wonders of Nature.

That this calcium business is true I was assured by experts – in other words Mothers – who had been Through It All and showed me their grey teeth to prove it. Being about to go Through It All myself at the time, I was ripe for education.

There were plenty of women prepared to tell me everything I wanted to know, and indeed a great deal that I didn't.

Varicose Veins (she showed me those too) told me to wear support hose and spend every afternoon with my feet up, as she would have done herself if she hadn't been too busy looking after other children. She had legs like old rope, and so would I if I wasn't careful.

Blood Pressure, whose personal hypertension shot the mercury practically out of the tube, had to spend eight months on her back in a darkened room, and even now was kept alive only by an amazing variety of pills. Though of course she'd been luckier than the girl in the next ward, who'd gone into a coma.

On the whole I'd have preferred her to have kept this story to herself, and instead told me something useful, if not actually cheerful – like the fact that disposable nappies aren't, and when flushed down the loos at airport lounges cause them to overflow. That was something I had to find out for myself.

Nor did anyone tell me that boy babies always pee on the wall just before you can get the nappy on, and that all babies reserve a portion of the last meal for dribbling on the mother's shoulder. (I think they have a special stomach for it, like cows).

No, they concentrated on the really *interesting* topics. The Le Boyer Method, Maternal Bonding, and the Importance of Fathers.

Maternal Bonding, by the way, is the ritual sticking of the baby to the mother's breast after birth, without which no mother and child can hope to have a stable, loving relationship. I expect it's because my daughter spent her first three days in a humidcrib that I never felt stable or loving while scraping her mashed pumpkin off the kitchen wall.

In case you're considering maternity yourself, I'll pass on a few tips from the experts.

Your behaviour depends on the prevailing fashion. If being an Earth Mother is In, you should be full of boundless energy, bloom like a rose, work like a Trojan throughout your pregnancy and have the baby as easily as shelling peas in between baking the bread and tie-dyeing your nightie.

In my day, the fashion was Stoic Frailty. The most admired pregnancy was that involving the most suffering, but only if it was done with silent stoicism. If you follow this fashion, you must of course let people *know* you have suffered, but this should be in the form of instruction to the uninitiated, after the event. Actually yelling one's head off during labour and threatening to personally sterilise one's partner is *not* done in the best circles. It is acceptable to *breathe* rather loudly, provided you do it in the proper rhythm.

Points are awarded for long labour (several days is best) breech births (extra points for No Anaesthetic) babies weighing over ten pounds, and haemorrhaging. This should necessitate the transfusion of several pints of blood, preferably of a rare group.

Caesareans are usually pretty good, if they are performed while the mother is conscious. Accepting a general anaesthetic shows a regrettable tendency to opt out of a Meaningful Life-Enhancing Experience.

In the early stages it is best to be sick as often as possible, preferably all day, or at least afternoons rather than mornings. Time off is allowed for Craving (usually in the middle of the night) but smoking and of course alcohol (except when nobody is looking) are Out.

As a pregnant woman, I wasn't a high achiever. I did manage to feel sick for a couple of months, though only in the mornings. I thought I was quite good at it – my knees got calloused from kneeling at the toilet bowl – but it was a poor performance by the current standards. By sheer effort of will I managed an occasional palpitation, and in the last weeks a mild case of toxaemia. But even then I was merely instructed to lie down for three days, and not even in a darkened room.

Of course there was still the delivery to get through, but I lost points there as well. It wasn't a Caesar, didn't happen in a taxi, and worst of all, the father wasn't present. As it happened neither was the doctor – he was playing golf – but it was the Father's absence that counted against me.

After we'd walked the hospital corridors for six hours and he was getting bags under his eyes, I sent him home to have a sleep and nipped in quick and gave birth in his absence.

It was a relief, really. I know I let the side down. I should have insisted on his partaking of the Complete Emotional Experience. But frankly I was reluctant to be seen belly-up with my feet strung up in the air, breathing rhythmically. I even told the nurses not to wake him up after the delivery, but they did, and he arrived just in time to hold my head over the vomit bowl.

'Of course, you wouldn't have *been* sick if you hadn't been gulping down all that gas!' said a friend afterwards. She's a natural childbirther herself and I know that, in her estimation, I don't measure up. But I don't care, really. After all, now I'm an expert, too.

Cows in the Night

There is no weariness like the weariness of a nursing mother. It is monumental, eternal, all-consuming. Her rest is not to be broken lightly. I speak from experience. Mine was shattered during a torrential downpour, three days after I'd brought my new son home from hospital. There was no father available to kick out of bed, either. He'd taken one look at his offspring and flown off to Europe, claiming that he had a conference to attend.

Ten minutes after I'd sunk into the abyss of sleep following the two o'clock feed, I was rudely plucked from it by a rhythmic clang! clang! clang! reverberating through the floor, and as I struggled desperately against consciousness I became aware of another sound accompanying it. Squooch. Squooch. Squooch. Someone in Wellingtons[1] appeared to be stamping about in the mud beneath our house while banging on the metal supports with a hammer. Temporarily galvanised by fury I leapt out of bed and flung open the window.

'What the *Hell* do you think you're *doing*?' I shrieked into the dark. There was a brief, panic-stricken silence.

Then 'MOOOOO!' came the reply.

Our bungalow was built on the side of a hill, so the back rooms were six feet above ground at the furthest point, and supported on metal poles. In the space beneath

---

[1] We simply called them rubber boots. Like Plimsoll, Wellington is a peculiarly British terminology.

the house we had builder's rubble, bits of fencing wire, and spiders. We had not planned on having cows there.

Pausing only to upend my boots in case they were harbouring deadly red-back spiders – even fury didn't eclipse the habit of a lifetime – I pulled them on and plunged out into the storm, dressed only in Wellingtons and a floral cotton nightie. It was one of those sudden thunderstorms that, after weeks of drought, deliver two inches of rain in an hour and turn the ground into a quagmire. I was drenched instantly. Water dripped from my hem and ran down my legs into my Wellies.

Lightning flashed, revealing the villains. They were only yearlings, and there was plenty of room for them under the house. They had wandered in from a neighbouring paddock, ignoring its feeble fencing, and taken refuge with us; amusing themselves by clanging their stubby horns on the poles and squelching their hooves in the mud. I pushed them each in turn on the rump and shouted 'Shoo!' They merely moved slightly further in and turned to look at me.

'Shoo!' I yelled, again, above the drumming of the rain. 'Go away! Clear off!'

And one or two other things that sprang to mind. They regarded me with their soulful brown eyes in that curious yet detached way that cows have, and completely ignored my commands. Perhaps I did lack authority, standing there with wet unkempt hair clinging to my face, wild-eyed and raving.

In frustration I stamped my feet, and realised at once why they wouldn't go. They thought I was one of them. With my sodden nightie clinging to my still cow-like figure, smelling of milk and stamping about in the mud, I must have seemed like a sister.

I turned away in the faint hope that curiosity might induce them to follow me out, but they weren't that stupid. It was wet out there.

There was still one avenue open to me however. I thought I knew their owner, and nothing, absolutely nothing, would give me greater satisfaction than to rout him out of bed at three a.m. and insist that he remove them instantly.

Across the valley was a small farm, and during the drought the cows had resourcefully found a way up through the bush to the longer, if not greener, grass on our patch. The farmer, who had a second job in town during the day, usually collected them when he returned in the evening.

It wasn't that we minded them having the grass, but they also ate the shrubs and saplings we were carefully keeping alive with the washing-up water. Even that was perhaps forgivable, but now things had definitely gone too far.

'Would you *kindly*' I began when he answered, 'remove your cows from beneath my house.'

I filled him in on the situation with the aid of a few choice and satisfying Australian adjectives.

He let me run on for several minute and then said, when I paused for breath, 'They aren't our cows.'

'How do you know?' I asked in disbelief.

'Because my wife – who incidentally isn't at *all well*, and was woken up by your phone call – do you realise that it is three o'clock in the morning? – has been to check while you've been talking. They're all here. In any case our cows have been de-horned. But I think I do know the owner, if you'll pause long enough to listen.'

There was, it transpired, a new neighbour, a policeman who had moved in while I'd been in hospital. He'd acquired two cows and some sheep in a bid for self-sufficiency. The farmer knew his name, but not his number. I should check with Directory Enquiries.

I can't recall why I didn't phone the real owner immediately. Perhaps Directory Enquiries was taking a tea break, or perhaps, having already vented my spleen, I was too drained to bother. Or perhaps it was because the baby, having slept like the dead through all the excitement, along with his sixteen-month old sister and their grandmother, now began to cry; with that peculiarly nerve wracking wail only a small baby can give.

By five o'clock all hope of sleep was gone, and having finally put the baby down I made some cocoa and sat up drinking it while the sun came up. My Mother-in-Law, a dairywoman herself and an early riser, joined me. She could have seen off a herd of heifers in the middle of the night without batting an eyelid. Unfortunately she was also deaf in one ear, and had been sleeping with her good ear to the pillow at the far end of the house.

At seven-thirty, by which time I was so bereft of adrenalin I was almost mild, I telephoned. It had stopped raining and the cows had moved from their night quarters to the front of the house, where they were breakfasting on dandelions. At about eight their owner came around with a rope and led them home.

I've never felt quite the same about cows since.

AFLOAT AT HOME AND ABROAD

'Look, Look!' I urged, 'There it is; *that's* the sort of house-boat *we* went on, on the river Murray.' And there it was in glorious colour, gliding serenely across our television screen with Russell Braddon looking lean and literate at the helm. 'A floating garage' was how he described it. A description fitting it with almost painful accuracy. We watched the last of BBC 2's *River Journeys*, this one down Australia's Mighty Murray, in the same sort of self-congratulatory atmosphere in which one watches a home movie. We too had navigated those waters, and *we* had done it when the river was in flood. Or rather three of us had – in the ten years since there had been an addition to the family.

'Is that the sort of boat you crashed into the gum tree?' asked my daughter. She had actually been with us at the time, but being only a year old had managed to sleep through the whole thrilling experience.

There is nothing quite as exciting as crashing a floating garage into a gum tree, in a gale. Not the sort of willowy eucalypt you might see in a Kew hothouse, either, but a massive river Redgum whose girth exceeded that of several elephants. The branches, correspondingly thick though they were, were being whipped about in the wind like bits of spaghetti, and the river, two miles wide, was heaving like a scene from *The Cruel Sea*.

At least, that's how *I* remember it – and I'll bet that's how the three children in the front cabin, wailing 'I want to go home! I want to go home!' remember it too. Not to mention their mother, who subsequently declined our invitation to go on the river again. She and her children had a full frontal view of the approaching impact. I was at the back, being Competent and Fearless, preparing to jump into the dinghy with her husband to help him get a rope around the tree and stop our progress into the midst of several motor boats moored at the foot of a cliff. My husband, at the helm, had decided to use what little steering we had to ram the tree; and somehow we did manage to tie up to it. In fact I tied the knot with such unnautical fervour that for a while it seemed we would be wedded to the tree permanently.

We had no steering because the engine had failed, having sucked several tonnes of willow leaves up its exhaust pipe and choked itself to death.

The houseboat was, as indicated, of that design which is more house than boat. Square, with no visible prow – a sort of luxury raft. So once the engine failed we were truly at the mercy of the elements, as directionless as a cork in a tornado.

It had been quite an eventful weekend from the start. Neither of the two families had ever been on a houseboat and the awful possibilities of losing toddlers over the side became apparent only after we were committed. Murray houseboats have extremely narrow side decking and very low, open railings. They also have a flat roof approached by a fixed ladder, ideal for adult sunbathing or children's suicide.

However, the weather (at first) was heavenly, and provided all children were in sight we quite enjoyed puttering along beside half-submerged telegraph poles and holiday shacks. It was on day two that malevolent fate struck.

The two men took the dinghy to do some fishing, and my husband's line caught on a snag. He jerked it rather too vigorously and the three-pronged saw-toothed hook leapt out of the water and buried itself in his hand. So, holding the injured hand behind his back, the better to display the gore to the passengers, he piloted us single-handed to the nearest settlement. He said it took his mind off the pain.

At Bowhill, which we reached in the early evening, the owner of the General Store loaned the men his battered Ute[1] – the springs had gone and so, they later discovered, had the headlights – for the forty-kilometre drive to the nearest hospital.

The doctor took a bolt-cutter to the shaft of the hook and somehow eased the prongs out, remarking that it made a change from removing shotgun pellets.

The following afternoon the storm blew up.

After that, I thought the holiday on the Narrowboat would be a snip. A week on the Grand Union canal, the perfect holiday for my visiting Australian parents. Seven sun-filled days slipping between banks of willow-herb, gliding under ivy-clad bridges and quaffing cider at quaint canalside pubs.

Well, the weather was good. But we hadn't allowed for the locks.

At least, my husband had, but his allowance was different from the rest of us. He calculated that we could spend all day going through locks and still have enough energy to play Scrabble after tea.

And he had. I, however, was shaking with fatigue, and my father was heard to mutter to my mother 'I think you'll have to take me home in a box, Edna.'

Locks, I discovered, are terribly simple devices designed for developing the biceps of narrowboaters. They are cunningly designed so that movement up or down the canal is impossible without their use, so that this exercise is an essential part of narrowboating.

Because locks have gates, and these must be opened by winding a winch. This is done using a windlass, a sort of

---

[1] Pronounced 'yoot'; short for 'utility truck'. A small pick-up truck.

metal handle, which sometimes flies off and hits you a sharp crack on the shin, and sometimes flies off and sinks without trace into the water, and eventually, after hernia-inducing efforts on the part of the operator, opens the paddles that allow the water levels to equalise. And after all that, the gates themselves must be opened by pushing on a bloody great wooden beam. And then the whole process is reversed to shut the gates after the boat has passed through. It's even more fun in the rain.

In many places there are long flights of locks one after another and it is possible to spend almost all day developing the biceps. The place that in others is occupied by biceps, in me is occupied by a flaccid, twitching, jelly. All I developed was chronic exhaustion.

When I finally agreed to try steering instead, I hit an oncoming boat. (I'd rather not go into it, if you don't mind. No one got hurt, though several people were severely startled).

Nevertheless, after two years rest we did it again – without my parents this time – and this time I steered the boat and *he* wound the locks. Now I know why he finds it easy to lock up and down all day, and I *think* he knows why I don't. Though he still seemed disgustingly fresh at the end of each day.

But we did stop at a few more canalside pubs this year. Last time he tended to forge past, crying:

'Onward, onward – it's only six hours till sunset and we've got to be at Chipping Norton[1] by Tuesday,' while my father and I gazed dolefully at the 'Crossed Keys' or the 'Jolly Boatman' with our tongues hanging out, and my mother made endless pots of tea in the galley. At locks she usually had just enough time to leap off and grab the odd postcard and a couple of bags of crisps for the kids from the lock shop, before we were off again.

---

[1] OK, I know Chipping Norton's not on a canal. I just like the name, alright? Maybe it was Market Bosworth. Stop being pedantic.

This second trip was much more relaxed, once I'd got over the initial terror of handling the boat. Whereas the Murray houseboat had been a garage, the narrowboat was more of a London Bus. *You* try steering a floating bus while standing on the back end and pushing the tiller in the opposite direction from the one your natural inclination tells you to. My husband only succeeded in getting me to do it at all by jumping off the boat and running off down the towpath towards the approaching lock, leaving me the choice of swimming (and abandoning the children to their fate) or grabbing the tiller. I grabbed, though weeping with fright.

After a week, though, I got almost used to it, though I never got the hang of entering a lock gracefully. I entered one so ungracefully that a pile of dirty dishes by the galley sink were flung to the floor and smashed by the impact. And I've lost count of the time I got the thing stuck on the mud through giving too wide a berth to oncoming traffic.

But I think if I ever come into money, I might just buy a narrowboat. With practice more regular than biennially, I might get to enjoy the boat, as well as the scenery.

AGENTS

My suburb is not famous for much except compost, but it's within walking distance of a rather upmarket part of Surrey. I went there recently to make enquiries on behalf of an Australian family who want a place to live while they're on sabbatical.

Shortly before my family and I left for the Land of Hope and Glory ourselves, a colleague sent us several estate agents' lists of places for rent. I had no idea of the truly heroic service she had performed in getting them.

I did not wear my hat with corks around it on Saturday, and I didn't take my swag. All I did was ask for a list of properties.

For rent.

'For yourself?' asked the lady at Toffs' Choice.

'No, for a family arriving from Australia next month.'

'I can't possibly say now what's going to be available next *month!*'

'That's quite alright – all they want is some idea of places and prices.'

'How long are they staying?'

'Four months.'

'We never let for less than a year. And only company lets. What firm is your friend with?'

I said he wasn't with a firm he was with a University. I did not get a list.

At Village Villas I was informed that the letting agent did not work on Saturdays, handed a card and ejected from the office in one fluid movement.

Still, I remained hopeful and telephoned on Monday morning with my request.

There was a brief silence before the agent asked, 'What sort of property are you interested in?'

'None,' I answered, 'It's for a family arriving from Australia soon.'

'Why *this* area, particularly?' I detected a faint distaste. I told her it was close to work.

'How long are they staying?'

'Some months,' I prevaricated.

'Well, raahlly, I don't see how I can help you.'

'All I want,' I said, 'Is a list of properties for rent!'

She gave an exasperated sigh.

'But unless we have some more *details* about the tenant we can't tell what would be suitable. We normally rent properties for at *least* a year. Very occasionally a property comes up for six months. If they wanted anything less it would be quite impossible.' I remained silent, and she added reluctantly, 'How many of them are there?'

'Five.'

'A four bedroom furnished house, then.'

'Or flat, and they might manage with two bedrooms.'

'None of *our* clients would *consider* allowing three children in one room. It would *have* to be at *least* three bedrooms. What rent were they considering?'

'I don't know,' I said.

'Well, we don't just give out *lists*. "Three bedroomed house, £150 per week", sort of thing.' I silently wondered how they had managed it five years earlier.

Suddenly a tone bordering on politeness entered her voice.

'Is he with the High Commission?'

'No, he's with a University in Western Australia,' I said, suppressing a desire to ask if she wanted his blood group and a copy of his family tree, and experiencing a powerful urge to scream.

'All I can suggest is that you send him along to our office when they arrive,' she said frostily, terminating the conversation.

I consulted the telephone directory, chose an area famous for riots and muggings, and confessed all to the first agent who answered. 'Family of five, arriving September, staying four months, would like details of properties available for rent; please could I have a list.'

This time the reaction was different. The girl at Cramped Cottages was almost – well – accommodating. 'Nothing for less than six months' she said, 'but I'll let you have a list anyway if you like.'

'Yes, please,' I said.

'Well, we have two lists, one starting at £450 a month and going up to 2000, and the other starting at 150 and going up to 450. Which would you like?'

'The lower one.' I said.

Howse and Holmes were positively sympathetic.

'We'd *love* to help,' they said, 'but even if they took out a six month lease, they'd be leaving in January, wouldn't they. And *nobody* wants to rent in London in January. And of course none of our clients would leave a house vacant for two months, for obvious reasons.'

Still, she sent me a list anyway.

'I'm afraid we don't do short lets,' said the girl at the next agency I phoned.

'But I've got your ad in the Gazette in front of me, and it says you do.' I said.

'Yes it *does*' she admitted, 'but we don't.'

One local paper listed a dozen flats for retired gentlewomen. Another had exactly two entries under rented accommodation, one of them beginning; 'Why rent, when you can buy?' A third offered country manors from 500 a week up.

But tucked away in the Miscellaneous column of the local free paper I saw the encouraging words 'House Finders, short and long lets. Telephone.'
I telephoned.
'Eh – oop?' answered a male voice.
'House Finders?' I asked.
'Aw, naw, naw loov. What noomber?' I repeated it.
'Oh, ah, thut's it.'
'Oh, sorry, ' I said. 'There must be a misprint in the paper.'
'Who were you wanting?'
'House Finders.'
'Oh!' Light seemed to dawn.
'Ah! Well, e i'n't in yet. 'E joost *died* y'see. 'E i'n't in yet.'

I was tempted to try again later, to see if he'd been resurrected, but I resisted.

We've written to the family concerned and broken it to them as gently as possible, that it's either a tent in our back garden or taking their study leave somewhere else – like at home.

BUTCHERS' RIGHTS

My local butcher is a likeable man, a man with a twinkle in his eye, and a pleasant line of chat. His figure is suggestive of steamed puddings and the roast beef of Old England. I feel that any frail old lady would be safe crossing a busy road on his arm.

And he has good meat. Some of it – lamb's tongues, livers – he feeds to his two dogs.

He was already at work cleaving a side of pork into chops when I arrived at eight one morning recently to talk to him.

'You're late!' were his first words. He'd probably been up at four, to be at Smithfield by five to buy his meat, which he does twice a week. He works long hours, and hasn't had a holiday since he was married, three years ago. It's not easy to get a locum. He has two helpers in the shop, a boy, and a woman who comes in part-time. I asked whether he knew any women butchers.

'I don't know any personally,' he said, 'But I do know of them – I've seen a few in the market.'

He's been a butcher for about twenty years – virtually all his working life – not through family tradition or particular ambition, but because a vacancy happened to be available. He learnt on the job.

'I didn't have an apprenticeship as such,' he told me. 'When I started in the trade it was a matter of you had to watch what was going on. Men wouldn't *teach* you – they were frightened for their jobs.' And if people stopped buying meat, I asked, what would he do?

'Join the dole queue' he replied. 'There's no jobs as it is, without increasing the unemployment.' He'd read in his trade paper that Smithfield, the central meat market, employs five thousand people.

'I mean, you take that away – just those five thousand – ' he said. 'It's a lot of people. I mean – there's got to be – ooh – there's got to be millions of butcher's shops. Say there's a million butcher's shops – and there's just one person in those shops – that's another million people in the dole queue.'

The most recent figures I could find on butchers were in the 1981 Government census, which numbers self-employed butchers at about thirty thousand.[1] Adding on butchers employed by others brings it up to something under a hundred thousand – or one thirtieth of the number of shops he guessed. But still a longish queue.

How easy would it be to sell the business if he wanted to? Difficult, he thought.

'There's more businesses going to the wall than holding' he said.

So it wouldn't be easy, even if he wanted to, for him to be anything other than a butcher.

Now, I suppose the argument that because something is difficult to change it should be allowed to continue could be used to justify anything from sweated labour to the Mafia. There are those who see butchering as little better than licensed cruelty, and want to be rid of it. But I don't think that putting a brick through my butcher's window – which is what I was there to talk to him about – is the best way to go about it.

---

[1] Between 1977 and 2001 the number of independent butchers shops fell from 25,300 to 8,344. But despite BSE, E-coli and Foot-and-Mouth we are still buying meat (mainly from supermarkets), and downing it like there was no tomorrow. Which, given Global Warming – in which bovine flatulence has, allegedly, a significant role – there may well be.

Indeed – and I admit to a personal interest here – I consider it the action of a fanatical and dangerous lunatic. It's destroyed any lurking sympathy I may have had for Animal Rights – that's Animal Rights with capital letters, by the way, the organization, not the concept. There is a difference, though you might not think it.

Of course there is only circumstantial evidence that my particular butcher's brick was thrown, as he says the police suggested, by an Animal Rights supporter. Their opinion was based on similar incidents where the perpetrators had identified themselves. No note was wrapped around this brick. Nobody daubed 'Butchers are Killers' in white paint on his walls, as they did a few streets away. Nobody put a bullet through his window, either. Just a brick.

'One of the shops down here,' he said, 'they reckon there was a shot through their window. The boy was standing in the shop, and it just missed his head. They could've killed that boy.'

Too right, they could have; or Mrs Smith who'd just popped in for her teatime chop. They could have brained one of my children with that brick, if they'd been walking past at the wrong moment. That's where my personal interest comes in. OK, I know that's emotive stuff, not the sort of reasoned logic one should use. It's difficult not to be infected by a group who are not above using emotive arguments themselves. My kids could be run over by a bus. Bus drivers, however, tend to avoid running people over if it's at all possible. Brick throwers – bomb-lobbers – and people who shoot through shop windows – are not noted for their consideration of innocent bystanders.

My butcher has a new window now. The breakage was covered by insurance.

So were the tyres someone drilled holes in at Smithfield market. Butchers' insurance premiums may go up a little. I wonder how many animals are saved by that?

There was a time when 'I'm just going to the butcher's for a pound of sausages' was not an inflammatory statement; and 'Militant Vegetarian' seemed a contradiction in terms. But times change. Even vegetarians may have to reconsider their positions before long. It has come to my notice that certain scientific advisors have expressed official concern about a current school science project on the grounds that 'it may cause distress to animals *and plants*'. The animals in question are shellfish and the plants, peas. They are being subjected to cigarette smoke during growth.

How soon can we expect the rise of militant pea-protectors? Should we start starving now – or may I murder just one more carrot?

ON BEING A GOOD CITIZEN

If somebody doesn't do something to resolve the strike soon, I shall be forced, to take action.[1]

I realised the other day that I had let things go on far too long. I should have stuck to my usual policy, which is to let a strike go on for a week before taking action, in the hope that it might all be over by then.

It hasn't worked, yet, but you never know.

The problem is that what with it having been so long since we've had any industrial unrest – it must be – what? – well, at least a fortnight – I've forgotten exactly what action it is that I should take, as a Concerned Citizen. So I had a look over my notes on the water workers strike, to see if I could find a few clues.

It has to be said that a lot of water has flowed under the bridge since the days when I sat hunched over a guilty cup of tea with the curtains closed, wondering when we were going to be told to boil all our drinking water. And who would tell us. Was it a job for the town crier, or did an Official Person drop a letter through the box? Should we go ahead and boil it anyway, just to be on the safe side? Or should we wait until it came from the tap with unspeakable objects floating in it?

At the time – two weeks into the strike – I wasn't boiling it (except for tea of course) but for a week I'd been

---

[1] Written in 1984, during the coalminer's strike.

doing my bit to save it. If it weren't that I naturally believe everything I read in the papers, I'd have been tempted to think that the water workers strike was a hoax. That on April the first all the newscasters would cry 'April Fool!' and we'd all discover we'd been recycling the hot-water bottle for nothing. Come to think of it, I hadn't heard of any of the places reported to be using standpipes and contemplating dried-up reservoirs. But I put that down to geographical ignorance. Anyway, I believed in them sufficiently to make an attempt to do the Right Thing.

It ought to be easy for Australians to save water; we're always running out of the stuff. I myself have eaten potatoes boiled in lemonade (and if you're wondering why we didn't just bake the potatoes and drink the Lemonade I can't tell you – but we didn't). As a child I gauged the level of water in the corrugated iron tank by banging on the side with a stone, and listening to it ring like a bell as the level sank rung by rung. As an adult I've lugged buckets of rinse-water from the washing to keep a vegetable garden alive.

But I've gone awfully soft since living in Britain. I've learned to love my bathtub; and the sound of a flushing toilet is music to my ears.

In fact where water was concerned I'd gone so soft I'd actually forgotten *how* to save it. When the papers advised us to put buckets out to collect rainwater I had to be *told* why. I knew it couldn't be for drinking purposes, because everybody knows – don't they? – that the water from London skies is so full of aviation fuel and sulphur dioxide it'd rot your guts quicker than a bottleful of gin. And that the reason Londoners carry umbrellas isn't so much to keep dry as to avoid acid burns. All those stone angels didn't lose their noses just from the sparrows perching on them.

No, the water was for flushing toilets. I'd already saved quite a bit simply by not reminding the rest of the family that they *should* be flushed; but after a week I decided it was time for more positive action. We would collect rainwater.

It was then that I discovered that our house was not built with the collection of water in mind. The downpipe from the guttering ended only inches above the drain. It might have been possible to fit a teacup under it, but my dedication did not extend to running up and down stairs all day with teacups full of water.

I allowed the matter to ride for a day, during which I succumbed to selfishness and washed my hair. I salved my conscience by washing it (my hair, that is) under the shower and treading a bathful of dirty washing at the same time. Later, swilling grease around the dishes in a small puddle of cooling washing-up water, I gave the matter further thought. The downpipe was made in sections, and sure enough, a firm tug removed the bottom section easily. It refused to go on again – indeed, two years later it is still held in place with a mouldering piece of sponge – but its removal made enough room under the pipe for a washing-up bowl.

It had obligingly snowed overnight, and while the freezing conditions were undoubtedly causing burst water pipes all over the country, I collected enough melt-water to fill a large plastic rubbish bin and a four gallon bucket. It was quite exciting seeing it mount up. A little deprivation brings out the best in all of us. I bounced up the stairs singing *Pack up your Troubles in your Old Kit Bag* and tied up the ballcock on the cistern, wishing I'd been in the habit of washing my windows so that I could feel saintly about not washing them now.

After three days, staggering upstairs with buckets of water began to pall, particularly since I had developed a filthy cold. It hadn't rained or snowed again either, and unless it did so quickly we'd be faced with the choice of using up community supplies or compulsory constipation.

Anyway, it occurred to me that either way, we were taking a stand in the dispute. If we saved water we prolonged the strike and supported the management; if we used it we hastened the breakdown of the system and supported the workers.

Being a convinced fence-sitter I decided to adopt an even-handed policy. I'd done my bit for Management. The next day I supported the workers; and had a bath.

And as you see, it worked. The water worker's strike is over, and we are once more nice to be near. Obviously in this present dispute, an even-handed policy is the answer.

When I've worked out just what, in this case, that is, I'll let you know.

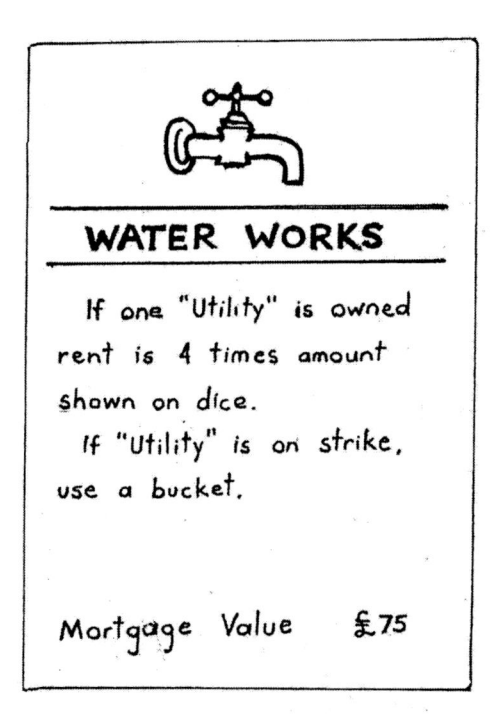

WATER WORKS

If one "Utility" is owned rent is 4 times amount shown on dice.
If "Utility" is on strike, use a bucket.

Mortgage Value £75

EDUCATION

' There is a certain type of middle aged, middle-class woman who becomes an Open University student...' These faintly damning words were uttered at an evening class I attended a couple of years ago. I cringed, and lowered my eyes. *I* was an O.U. student. Well, almost. I had enrolled. But the academic year had not yet begun. Perhaps it was not too late to withdraw? But I wasn't middle aged. At least only just. And anyway, I needed the degree. All my acquaintances were conspicuously Educated, and my inferiority was giving me a complex.

Coming from a long line of academic snobs, I've always been a sucker for Education – school, Poly, Further Ed., – you name it. Mind you I've always felt a bit furtive about being a Mature Student, which is a bit like living in Milton Keynes – not something you admit in mixed company.

The class in which I heard the remark about female O.U. students was called *Writing for Pleasure and Profit.* My own motives for joining were partly to meet people (I was new to the country) and partly to discover whether it was actually possible to make any money by writing.

I discovered that it was, but not for me. Nevertheless, although there was no profit – indeed there was a positive loss, in money spent on paper and postage – there was a great deal of pleasure. When one of the class had a story accepted by the BBC we felt a collective thrill, and her letter of acceptance, passed from hand to hand, gave us all new hope. We read our work to the class in the slightly cowardly knowledge that its criticism would be kind, bringing out poems and half-finished novels we'd hidden, like illicit whisky, at home. In fact it looked as though I might complete the course without incident, until the optional residential weekend came up.

I had not yet fully realised that it takes at least three times as long to travel anywhere in London as in Adelaide. This, and the fact that I stood at the wrong bus stop for more than half an hour, meant that I arrived after dark, two hours late, and incurred the wrath of the warden.

'WHO' he thundered, 'are YOU?'

I quavered apologetically.

'You're VERY LATE!' he accused. 'Your knocking has completely destroyed our train of thought. WHO did you say you were?' He made no allowance for my thoughtfulness in *not* knocking on the French windows of the library, where I had observed the other residents deep in composition. Had I done so, half of them would probably have dropped dead on the spot.

At the risk of being savaged by fierce guard dogs, I had traversed the dark garden to the main entrance, and used the massive doorknocker.

I would have bolted on the spot had not a friend appeared and announced that we were to be room mates. She had also arrived late, but had discovered an open back door and so avoided the warden's ire. She showed me to our room and thence to an anteroom near the library where we were to wait for the class to finish. This gave me ample time to mull over the dreadful possibilities of a whole week-end spent with fifty people who took the Muse so seriously that a mere knock on the door could destroy it. On the pretext of fetching some notes I returned to the bedroom, picked up my case and crept out into the night, leaving a note of apology – and my nightie – behind me.

I should have known right from the start that education and I were incompatible.

In infant school I was the only child in third grade that couldn't tie her shoelaces. Mine were the knickers that fell down in front of the class. I it was who lovingly planted a weed in the school garden, when everyone else planted a seedling. I couldn't even learn to make paper gum-blossoms.

Paper gum-blossoms must be about the easiest flowers on earth to make. You take a fringe of red crepe paper, roll it up and fasten it to a green stem – and there you are. Except that when I did it, it looked like a piece of tattered rag on a wire. When I was reduced to tears the little boy next to me made one for me. I will never forget him.

I needed the paper gum-blossom to wave at the Queen. She was on her first Royal tour of Australia at the time, and each South Australian school had its allotted place at the Adelaide showgrounds, from which to watch the royal procession. Boys were to wave Union Jacks, and girls, gum-blossoms. At the approach of the regal Rolls, boys were to bow, and girls to curtsey. We had been practising at school for weeks, but somehow I couldn't master curtseying. I don't know how it is possible to curtsey incorrectly, but I did it so consistently that a frustrated teacher hit me about the legs with a ruler. *The* Ruler I never saw. On the appointed day, I was at home with bronchitis.

Even now I have an occasional nightmare in which I am presented to Her Majesty and, in curtseying, back into a Royal Object d'Art and send it crashing to the throne-room floor. That's why I keep a low profile. I wouldn't want to do anything I might get a medal for.

It was that Royal tour that aroused my latent ambition. I passionately wanted to be a Wattle Blossom. (Native flora featured heavily at the royal tour). Wattle Blossoms (Mimosa to you) were little girls in beautiful yellow and green silk dresses, who performed the Wattle Dance, especially created for the occasion, before the royal party.

They practised daily in the schoolyard and my envy was acute. I was only six, and perhaps I wasn't old enough to join them. But it was more likely to have been because I couldn't curtsey – let alone dance. Always a wall-flower, never a wattle blossom – that's me.

The trouble is I still *want* to be a wattle blossom. Unrealised ambition gnaws at my vitals. So I go on trying. Chemistry, art, spinning and weaving, I've tried them all. And I keep trying, in bursts, with pauses in between to lick my wounds, in the hope that some day I might discover something that I can do. Something that I can qualify as. I don't suppose I ever will – but as somebody said, it's better to travel hopefully than to arrive.

OF CLASS AND CLASSICS

Certain Englishmen make me nervous. There are some Englishwomen too, but fewer of them. Perhaps, being of the same sex, I feel that we have at least one thing in common. But men; well, they're practically a different breed, aren't they? Particularly English men of a certain type.

I had a brief encounter with one the other day in a music shop in Dover Street. Now Dover Street is close to Bond Street, in that area of London where everything in the shop windows looks as though it could only be happy with a person of breeding, and even the people in the street look beautiful. So, having sneaked along behind a ravishing red woollen cloak and a stunning pinstripe (female) trying to appear inconspicuous in my baggy cords and jumper, I was already somewhat demoralised when I entered the shop. Or showroom, as it was less commercially called. And there he was. Behind the counter. I recognised the type instantly. Young, slim, large eyes, long thin nose for looking down. Pale, prehensile fingers. Etiolated I think is the word though I'm probably pronouncing it incorrectly.

He, on the other hand, would almost certainly have pronounced it correctly, as indeed any other word thrown at him, including 'Divertimenti'. 'Divertimenti' is a word I find rather difficult to say, especially when my salivary glands have ceased to function, as they usually do in the presence of such a person. They woke up and began working at top speed just as I opened my mouth, causing me to spit at him.

'Could I have,' – I licked my lips – 'Mozart's four Dementi... I mean Demen...' I stopped, and with a supreme effort of concentration said. 'Diver-ti-menti' very slowly, like a drunkard. 'For three clarinets.' And grinned. He did not return my grin (they never do) but said pityingly 'Do you want the scores or the parts?'

'Both.' I said rashly.

He raised his eyebrows a fraction, and turning to the telephone behind him requested them to be sent up. Then he told me the price.

'Can I change my mind?' I asked. He shrugged delicately.

'They'll come up anyway,' he said. 'You can decide then.' As he spoke they arose from beneath the floor in a sort of dumb-waiter operated by a rope and pulley. I was impressed.

'What a useful contraption' I remarked. Perhaps this might raise some sign of enthusiasm, some indication of fellow feeling? But no.

I decided to take the scores only, and put them into my shopping bag while he was at the till. He was disconcerted.

'Oh ' he said. 'I was going to give you a bag. Oh well, never mind.'

Obviously I was beyond redemption. I wasn't even a plastic bag carrier. I escaped with relief; and imagined him reporting my eccentricity to the gnome in the basement.

Music shops are particularly likely places for this sort of embarrassment because, even before I open my mouth, I feel that the staff can tell just by looking at me that I'm not a genuine musician.

'Couldn't tell a basso from a profundo' I can feel them thinking. And then when I *open* my mouth...

Of course what we're really talking about is *class*. I've never really known what class I belong to. Even in

Australia I had trouble, at least after I married. Here I'm totally confused. I think I'm probably a Lower Class Snob. 'Lower' rather than 'working' in my case, because I don't do anything that could properly be called 'work'. My accent, I suspect, brands me as a yob and my background is definitely 'working'. However, I happen to have married an academic, and it appears that here, as in Australia, to be an academic confers a sort of Middle-Class halo even on those of doubtful origin. Consequently, from time to time I am thrown together with people whose spouses are Executives in Industry and who go to places like Bordeaux for lunch; people who have hyphenated names and buy their shoes in Italy, and can read poetry in public without embarrassment. They are usually either devastatingly beautiful or interestingly ugly, and are capable of producing witty remarks without appearing to have practised them in the bath beforehand.

It's usually at these affairs that I meet the few women who make me nervous. I once met one who had actually been to a Swiss finishing school (I thought they existed only in novels). Her peaches-and-cream complexion was perfection and her upper-crust accent impeccable, at least to my antipodean ear. It was at the same party that I was officially, so to speak, classified by one of the male guests who had spent some time in Australia. We were discussing the variations in the class systems in our respective homelands.

'And I would say,' said he, 'judging by your accent, that you were *not* from the highest class – if you don't mind my saying so.'

Not from the highest Australian class, he meant; that being the one comprising those people whose accent most closely approximates Educated English; the sort that only a private school education can produce. He was quite right, of course; but I did mind him saying so. Though I despised myself for minding, as I despise myself for being ashamed of my Australian accent among the English. But I *am* ashamed of it. After all, if you're subtly indoctrinated from the cradle with the idea that your speech and culture is inferior to the English, eventually you come to believe it.

I personally cannot even claim to be of pure English stock; my ancestry being a mixture of English, Scots, Dutch and Austrian, with possibly a smidgen of Polynesian thrown in, judging by youthful photographs of one of my relatives. I don't even have the distinction of having sprung from convict stock, which I think is still pretty trendy in Australia.

Being such a jumble of genes and a confusion of cultures, I think I'll have to settle for being in a class by myself. I might even get myself a T-shirt with that phrase printed across the front, for wearing in the presence of certain types of English persons.

Though on second thoughts, that might be even more embarrassing.

THE JOYS OF LITTLE CHILDREN

'The Joys of Little Children,' as my mother often says, 'are grossly overrated.' Probably she says it less often than she used to, now that her most troublesome child – me – is twelve thousand miles away, but I'm sure her silence is one of relief rather than regret.

'I used to think that being married would be wonderful,' she once told me. 'A man's whole wage packet to spend, and nothing to do all day but play with a dear little pink baby. And then you came along.'

I was a disappointment from the start, being not pink, but blue. This was a terrible nuisance because it meant not only frequent visits to doctors (which at least got us out of the house) but also frequent visits from my aunt, who came to make sure that her brother's child was being looked after properly and to run her fingers along the edges of the door frames looking for dust. Her first action, after checking that I was still breathing, was to walk around the house pulling down all the blinds, to prevent the sunlight from fading our carpets. Mum resented auntie because she had been to Teachers' College and had taught in a high school for a year, before marrying a farmer and becoming a member of the landed gentry.

She considered Mum vulgar and uneducated because she was the fifth of thirteen children and had left school at the age of ten to pull onions in Grandpa's market garden.

My maternal Grandmother, in spite of having had thirteen of them (or perhaps because of it) didn't seem to be too keen on children either. When driven to distraction she would put her hand around the offending child's throat and cry 'I'll *swing* for you one day!'

Or so my mother tells me. Her own favoured weapon was the wooden spoon.

Mostly, though, she simply shut us inside and escaped into the garden.

Another escape-route from the demands, accusations and recriminations of her children was singing. An innocent childish remark such as 'Why do *I* always have to do the dishes? Geoffrey never has to do the dishes!' was enough to make her burst into song, usually beginning with

You Can't Come and Play in our Yard, I Don't Like You Any More, and proceeding through *Barney Google, with the Goo-Goo-Googley Eyes*, which I particularly hated, to *In My Sweet Little Alice Blue Gown*, which she sang so affectingly she sometimes made herself cry. If she simply felt like singing, as she occasionally did, she often sang *Now Honey, You Stay in Your Own Back Yard*, which I hated even more than *Barney Google*, because it made *me* cry.

There is just no defence against this weapon. If we yelled, she simply sang louder.

'I could have been a professional singer if I hadn't had you children,' she told us. 'I could have been an actress. I could have been anything. But no – I'm stuck in this God-forsaken hole with you battening on me like leeches.'

Then she would turn dramatically from the kitchen sink and declaim:

'Full many a flower is born to blush unseen,

And waste its sweetness on the desert air.'

Mum definitely considered that she was wasting her sweetness on the desert air, which was particularly appropriate as the God-forsaken hole we were living in at the time was a fruit-growing town on the Murray River, and a mile or two away from the orange groves there was nothing as far as the eye could see but sheep, saltbush, and red sand dunes loosely held together by spinifex. There was always enough water to keep the garden going though. I expect the fact that the septic tank overflowed regularly helped.

Mum was spending more time gardening than ever, and singing even louder, because Geoffrey, who was seven, always seemed to be kicking his football into somebody's yard and breaking a treasured plant, two-year old Richard seemed intent on seeking out baby brown snakes and redback spiders in the wood heap, and I was developing a bust and trying to sneak off to school without a bra.

Worse than puberty, however, was my announcement that I intended to choose Latin and science when I started High school the following year because I had decided to be a doctor. My mother's reaction was extreme.

'No daughter of mine is going to be a doctor!' she said. 'Nobody will marry a woman doctor. All women doctors end up as queer old maids.'

It was probably already apparent to her that I might not make good marriage material, and the prospect of me living at home forever rendered her incapable of looking at the problem rationally. It apparently didn't occur to her that did I succeed in my ambition I would earn enough money to be able to leave home. My father was much more reasonable.

'Just leave it alone, woman!' he said. 'She'll need a scholarship to go to University anyway, and she won't get that.' As it happened he was right. But Mum and I feuded for five years anyway.

Between fights I sat up in the pepper tree in our garden and planned a future that included no husband or children and Mum sat in the kitchen smoking and writing her alternative life history inside her head. When she was out of cigarettes she would send me down to the chemist's for a packet of over-the-counter sedatives. To such remedies are we unmaternal mothers reduced.

When I had children of my own I found that the greatest advantage of living on a large isolated block of land was being able to go outside and scream at the top of my lungs; knowing that nobody would come to take me away. Though I often wished they would.

Washing nappies one day, with tears of self pity coursing down my cheeks, I found myself singing

'Curly Locks, Curly Locks, wilt Thou be Mine?

Thou shall not wash Dishes, nor yet feed the swine...'

That was when I knew what Heredity is all about.

HATS

The first time I consciously noticed how beautiful my mother was, she was wearing a hat. It was a stiff beret of emerald green felt, with a small bunch of green feathers fastened at one side by a piece of jet. I don't remember whether it had a veil, but probably it did – veils were fashionable then. There was certainly a veil on the other hat I remember her wearing. That was a shiny black straw that had to be anchored with a hatpin. The veil was also black, with a scattering of little bobbles. If I stared at her through narrowed eyes the thin web would dissolve, leaving her slightly out-of-focus face covered with black spots. Behind the veil, her face seemed to be in a cage. Once, she drank a cup of tea through it. Or at least I think she did – but perhaps that's just wishful thinking. Memory is a terrible liar.

If she actually did, then we were probably having afternoon tea at Balfours. Balfours was Adelaide's version of Lyons; and having tea there made up a little for the awful tedium of an afternoon spent watching my mother trying on hats. Hats were the delight of her life, and the bane of mine. I was pre-school, and it was the Fifties, when Australian women *wore* hats. And gloves. Mum wore them to hide her hands, which were big and bony and covered with sunspots. When they went out of fashion she regretted them even more than hats, but looking at her hands depressed her, and consequently we never spent long at the glove counter. She did occasionally *buy* gloves though. Hats, she just tried on.

They were usually too expensive for a family on the breadline. 'The breadline' was a pretty vague concept to a four year old. It was a term redolent of the warm yeasty perfume of the bakers cart; but I knew that those of us on it had to 'live on the smell of an oily rag', which seemed contradictory. At any rate, hats were a luxury. Perhaps that's why, in the lean post-war years, they gradually went out of fashion.

But while they were still normal wear my mother would scrape together ten shillings out of the housekeeping over a period of weeks, and off we would go to town. The best part was getting there. In those days Adelaide had its own red British double-decker buses, and with luck we might ride on top, though this didn't happen as often as I would have liked. Mum would have been expecting her second child about then and climbing the stairs could have been hazardous. I think she had a craving for hats, the way other women crave pickles. The visits to town certainly became less frequent when my brother arrived. Perhaps there was less money, or hats were already fading from the scene.

They were still the rule in Church though. I was even made to wear one during my brief time at Sunday school. It was fluffy pink velour with a pom-pom at the back, which boys behind me tugged surreptitiously throughout the lesson. The irritation may account for my subsequent scepticism.

By the time I was twelve, hats were not considered an absolute necessity even in church, at least not C of E. However, when I arrived hatless at a cousin's Catholic wedding my aunt was so affronted that she insisted that I either wear one of her own hats or remain outside the church. Reluctantly, I chose the former, and spent the ceremony hunched in the pew, balancing her too-large, tulle-swathed beige straw on my glowering brows.

The grandest headgear I've ever worn was a brocade turban with an enormous glass jewel in front, made for me by my mother as part of my costume in the school Nativity play. In this, and a green velvet cloak, I was the grandest of the three wise men. Reverently I knelt before the Holy family proffering my cardboard box of simulated Myrrh; and bowed my head. Imperceptibly (at first) the turban tilted, and aided by the nervous sweat of my brow, slid slowly over my eyes and came to rest on the bridge of my nose. Refusing to call further attention to myself by removing it, I remained in blind supplication throughout the scene, burning with shame at the giggles of the audience.

At High School I was forced to wear one of those awful wide-brimmed straw hats, which I loathed with a pure hatred. It was prickly, it got in the way, and if I wore it with an elastic strap it half strangled me. Without the strap it blew off and got trampled underfoot. *And* it represented Authority.

In order to uphold the public dignity of the school students were required to wear full uniform while travelling to and from it. Of course most of us removed our hats as soon as we were out of sight of the buildings, and those of us who rode bikes didn't even go that far – they only blew off as soon as we got up speed. In my first year a particularly officious Prefect, who had recently acquired an ancient Morris Minor, pursued me and a friend half-way home, forced us off the road in true Gestapo style and gave us each a week's yard duty.

I would like to report that she got her comeuppance; unfortunately she won every scholarship going and when last heard of was an outstanding member of the medical profession. I'll bet there are no malingerers in *her* waiting-room.

Hats have never been lucky for me. They don't look right and they never fit, and they make me feel conspicuous and awkward. I want to melt into a crowd, not stand out in it. (Well, most of the time). But now hats seem to be coming back into fashion, and when I see some slim elegant creature sporting a chic little curve of velvet on her perfectly groomed head, or a Greer Garson type in something soft with a downturned brim, I feel a twinge of half regretful envy. If only things had been different... But no. Some women are born to wear hats, and some aren't.

I guess the only sort for me is the practical sort. One that keeps the sun off. And has a brim hung with corks on strings, to keep away the flies.

Hair

I've just returned from the hairdressers. I still feel like a lobster from the hairdryer. It was wonderful. I haven't had my hair done professionally for almost fifteen years. *That* was on my wedding day, when I considered it prudent to look as glamorous as possible in case my prospective husband changed his mind at the altar.

I have long, brown, very straight hair, which I wear in a ponytail except on special occasions when I pin it up in a plait. So I don't need a hairdresser, and I wouldn't have gone today if my husband hadn't won me a free hairdo in a raffle at the local school fete.

We've done quite well out of school fetes – the odd bottle of pop, an Airfix model that nobody could put together, a money box shaped like a football boot, still barren two years on. We never win the life-size plush panda, but we live in hopes. This year my daughter won a bottle of Babycham. We all had a thimbleful to celebrate Daddy's winning me a hairdo. The children were over the moon about it. You'd think he'd won a weekend for two at Claridges, complete with champagne breakfast.

'Mummy, Mummy!' They'd yelled, falling all over themselves with excitement, 'Look what Daddy won you!' and they handed me a pastel coloured card bearing the words 'Shampoo and set or blow-dry, Diana's of Grand Drive.'

'Well...' I began, looking at Daddy, who had what I can only describe as a funny look on his face – 'It isn't really *me*, is it? I think I should give it to Ann, or Denise, don't you? *They* go to the hairdresser quite often.'

Their faces fell.

'Oh, go on; *please*! They might make it all spiky and put pink dye in it!' giggled my daughter.

'Ugh; She'd look like a punk rocker!' exclaimed her brother in disgust. He's a hopeless conservative.

'I think they'd have to cut it to do that, and there's nothing on the card about cutting. Just a shampoo and set.' The idea of me at the hairdressers was almost as incongruous as Cyril Smith at an aerobics class. 'Besides, what's the point of having my hair done just to do the weekly shopping? People have their hair done to *go* somewhere. And I've had my birthday.' But I was weakening. It *would* be an Experience, and Experiences are all grist to the mill of we writers. And since I wasn't going down the Amazon in a canoe or crossing the Andes in any balloons before Christmas, I might as well have my hair done.

Besides, I'd just remembered that we *were* going out on the following Friday. So with any luck I could make the appointment then.

I had no idea what they could do with my hair, except perhaps fluff it out into those loose romantic waves models wear in shampoo commercials. In which case I'd need a face-lift as well. As I approached the shop at the appointed hour I wondered whether hairdressing establishments had changed much in the last fifteen years.

They haven't. Or not at Diana's, anyway. Behind the lace-curtained windows was the same atmosphere of warm lacquer-perfumed air, the same ladies toasting under the same beehive-shaped driers, the same piles of *Vogue* and *Woman's Realm*. Even the problems on the problem pages were the same. Only the face – mine – had aged. On the other hand, I'm more used to it. I didn't experience the same shudder of horror at my reflection that used to come over me in younger days when I visited the hairdresser more often. Perhaps they've done something to the mirrors. Or I've achieved resignation.

I'd always wanted hair that was long enough to sit on, but no such luck. It stops just below my shoulder blades, but even that was enough to be remarked on by the by the blue-smocked girls at Diana's, who all have short curls.

Apparently long hair is terribly old-fashioned, unless you happen to be Lorraine Chase, as who wouldn't be.

After I'd been washed, rollered, and cooked under the drier with my *Woman's Realm* until I felt ready to burst into flames, the staff stood around watching the boss teasing and pinning. I felt rather like a hospital patient whose unusual symptoms are being demonstrated to a group of medical students.

'They didn't teach us about long hair at College,' remarked the assistant handing the hairpins. 'They say there's no call for it nowadays.'

'I like doing long hair myself' said the boss. 'I think it looks nice piled up. I hope your husband's taking you out to dinner,' she added, to me.

We aren't going out to dinner; but a Royal Institution lecture is quite a glamorous occasion. Evening dress is worn, and the audience is full of distinguished academics in silver hair and black ties, and elderly ladies in velvet who look as if they might have known Marie Curie personally. Even I wear my long skirt and dangly earrings. So it's an appropriate outing for a posh hairdo. And you do get a cup of coffee afterwards.

When I left, the children suggested I take a camera and a friend to take a photograph before I left the shop, to prove I'd actually had something done. It was pouring down outside and a Force Four gale was whipping umbrellas inside out along the High Street. The sort of wavy blow-dry I'd expected would have fallen out immediately I stepped out of the door, but the girls had pulled out all the stops and I was finished off with enough lacquer for several Japanned boxes.

I really felt that it looked quite pleasing – piled up into three smooth loops at the back, with a couple of corkscrew curls at the sides. When I opened the door to the children on their return from school, I felt almost like Cinderella.

They were completely frank.

'*Ooh-er* – it's *horrible*!' They chorused. '*Horrible!*'

'You look like E.T., Mum!' said my son.

'It's so *old fashioned*!' said my daughter. 'You didn't walk down the *street* looking like that, did you? It's so old *fashioned*!' she repeated. 'Take it down!'

'Yes, yes, take it down!' echoed her brother. 'Ugh!'

When I pointed out that it was perfectly in keeping with what the more octogenarian members of the Royal Institution would be used to, my daughter admitted grudgingly that it *might* look a bit better without the tracksuit bottoms and Daddy's old High School blazer.

Now there's a thought. It was very cold this morning and before I left I put on a tight polo-necked shirt and a round-necked jumper. I wonder how I'm going to get them *off* without dismantling the whole structure?

GOD REST YE MERRY, GENTLEPERSONS

My best friend rang me up a while ago to tell me the latest horror story from school. She's a new teacher. This is her first job, and though she's had plenty of experience in what some people like to call The University of Life, I don't think anything quite prepared her for sixty pre-schoolers.

Her tales of woe always take up about an hour and I have to hiss at the children to go and turn the gas off so that whatever's bubbling in the cauldron doesn't boil dry, whenever she rings up. This one concerned Hassan, who thinks he's The Incredible Hulk. Apparently Hassan was in the Wendy House, terrorizing a couple of little girls, when...

'Oh dear! I don't mean the Wendy House. I mean the... oh what is it... the Play House.' Friend corrected herself, guiltily. 'Sorry, I forgot. We're not allowed to call it the Wendy House any more.'

'Why not?' I asked.

'Well,' she mused, 'It's got to be either racist or – you know –'

'Sexist?' I suggested.

'Yes,' she said. 'Which do you think it is?'

I must admit I was stumped for a minute. After all, Wendy was white. And middle class. Perhaps it was Classist? No, too subtle, I thought.

It has to be sexist, doesn't it? I mean, you didn't see Peter Pan wasting time tucking the Lost Boys up at night and playing Mother-Substitute, did you? No, he was out in the Real World (well, sort of) Having At Captain Hook with his trusty blade, as I recall. I also seem to recall that he had one or two unpleasant characteristics – something to do with congenital lying – but it is a long time since I read the book. I must have another look at it.

Anyway, *they*, whoever they are, hadn't sent out a directive to call it a Peterhouse. Or even a Wendy-and-Peterhouse. Well, they couldn't, really, could they, because that would have led to problems of precedence. Is it a Wendy-and-Peterhouse or a Peter-and-Wendyhouse? Far too confusing. So, sensibly, in my view, they opted for unvarnished Play House. Which probably means that for generations to come it will be called the Wen-playhouse.

We don't have this problem in Australia. I did try to keep Australia out of it, honestly. But the fact is we call them Cubby houses, I don't know why. Perhaps it's short for cupboard, because that's about the size of it. Or it could be Cub, of course, as in young animal. Or junior Boy Scout. There's scope for a bit of sexism there, if the committee's interested.

After Friend had got the Hulk incident off her chest and unburdened herself of the guinea-pig fatality and the finger-crushed-in-the-play-apparatus, she asked me if I'd be willing to bring my clarinet around one day and play a few nursery rhymes, as music hadn't been her strong point at college and her team teacher, who played piano, was off sick.

I agreed to go if she gave me a bodyguard and a list of ideologically acceptable compositions.

I had thought of playing a few Christmas carols, since it was about that time of year, but it could have been a minefield. I didn't think the infants would mind, but I had a feeling that They – the Committee for Uprooting Racism and Sexism in Education – would be down on us like a ton of bricks.

Apart from the Religious Imperialist overtones, it would probably be more than her job was worth to introduce into the classroom a song with the blatantly sexist title 'God Rest Ye Merry, Gentlemen.' What about the women? Well, we all know where they were supposed to be, don't we? Perspiring gently over a hot stove, mulling the wine and mincing the pies, and generally waiting hand and foot on the men. Of course if they were genuine upper-crust *Gentle*women they would probably be elevated to merely supervising the lower orders of their sex in the task – but either way, it's hardly the role model we want for our three year olds, is it?

And while we're about it, isn't it about time somebody told The Incredible Hulk it's his turn to make the sandpies and wash up the dolls' teaset?

FISHING FOR MILTON KEYNES

For most of this year my brain has had pride of place among the bric-a-brac on our dresser.

'Come and see mummy's brain!' the children cried, dragging in reluctant visitors. But it wasn't my brain really – it belonged to the Open University at Milton Keynes. And it was only half a brain. The left half, in durable pink plastic, complete with removable cortex and cerebellum.

When the Home Experiment Kit arrived it was like Christmas all over again.

The whole family gathered at the opening and each took turns dismantling Mummy's brain – something they've been doing for years, come to think of it – and reassembling it.

After the initial enthusiasm, however, the brain was left to gather dust among the Christmas cards in favour of the other component of the home experiment kit, the tropical fish tank. Complete with instructions on the purchase and care of *Betta splendens*, the Siamese Fighting Fish.

The children were a bit disappointed that I was requested to provide only one (male) fish, but one fish, like half a brain, is better than none. They also rather fancied a deep-sea diver with bubbles coming out of his helmet, and some waving waterweeds, but such luxuries were not permitted. Nothing was allowed to distract the fish from his appointed task, which was to swim through hoops.

My task was to determine whether my fish could discriminate between blue and green. For this purpose the kit contained red, blue and green plastic-coated wires, hoops for the making of.

No red-blooded male fighter can be expected to go through hoops for nothing. It has to be rewarded for correct performance, with freeze-dried tubifex worms. A note of caution was sounded in the experimental guidelines here.

It was going to be necessary at some point for the fish to perform its act about a hundred and fifty times in succession, and even the most cooperative fish, if stuffed to the gills long before this figure was reached, might lose interest in the proceedings. If we wished to use it, there was a non-fattening alternative, the mirror.

Siamese fighters, the notes said, will eagerly put on an aggressive display to their own reflections, just as they will at the sight of another male fish.

The family watched expectantly while I tested our fish's reactions, and he performed beautifully, erecting his gorgeous fins with admirable ferocity.

'OOH! OOH! Do it again!!' shrieked the observers with delight, jumping up and down and causing the fish to flee to the protection of the immersion heater.

I read them the notes about our Nearest and Dearest fouling up scientific accuracy, and warned them that anyone caught sneaking the fish a look at himself out of hours would suffer dire consequences.

Using the mirror worked like a charm, at first. I had just got the fish to the stage of nudging a tentative nose through the red hoop when he developed an acute case of mirror-phobia.

Instead of greeting his reflection with a macho flex of the muscles he took to darting away to the farthest corner of the tank, quivering visibly.

The notes had mentioned this possibility, but said it was nothing to worry about. Give your fish a day off, they said, and next morning it will be as right as rain.

It wasn't. It was still sulking in a marked manner a week later.

A change of tactics was indicated, but this presented a problem, because it wouldn't eat dried worms. I'd tried wiggling them about on the surface, I'd starved the fish for two days and tried again, I'd even read it the label on the container, which assured me that it would practically eat from my hand. It continued to treat the stuff with contempt.

On the tenth day it died of starvation.

It wasn't an encouraging start, but we O.U. students are made of stern stuff. I discovered an aquarist who sold live tubifex worms, and had a beautiful, mermaid-coloured blue-green fighting fish for sale.

Live worms, I also discovered, are easy to pick up singly with a medicine dropper. Fish number two, on Task Reinforcement Day, swam through the red hoop ninety-two times for as many worms before retiring, considerably bloated, to sleep it off. I reckoned that was good enough, and we proceeded to Phase Two, Blue-Green discrimination.

I'm sure it was perfectly aware that it was fed only for swimming through the green hoop. I think it simply wasn't bothered. After all, it had nothing else to do with its time. It realised, I'm sure, that if it swam through a hoop – any hoop, any colour – eventually it would get a feed.

Sometimes it hung in mid-water between the two hoops, glancing around to make sure I was still watching. Once it hung for several minutes with one fore fin resting on either side of a hoop, before backing out again. The assignment cut-off date was rapidly approaching, and I had to submit my results and concluded that either I was a failure as an animal trainer or my fish was colour-blind.

In October, the Home Experiment Kit – minus fish – had to be returned to the university. I was spared the moral dilemma of choosing between callously disposing of my faithful fighter, or buying him his own fish tank. Two weeks after I'd submitted my results, he died. I don't know why. Perhaps it was boredom.

It cast a little pall of gloom over the whole assignment.

I think I'll do the Nineteenth Century Novel next year.

Dunnies

I was very impressed by a scheme that was mooted in about 1984, two years before Halley's Comet was due to return to view, to turn the domestic toilet into an astronomical observatory, complete with simulated night sky and recorded commentary on the motions of the planets. It sounded wonderful – if rather expensive. Of course those lucky enough to possess an outdoor loo can observe the real thing any clear night they feel the call, through the gap above the door – or even the holes in the corrugated iron roof.

Though lacking the expert commentary, such an edifice has its own sound effects – the howling of dingoes at the dog-proof fence, the bloodcurdling cry of the curlew, (or bunyip as it is affectionately called), the persistent scuffle of small unidentifiable creatures in the dark. I am of course referring here to the Australian outdoor loo, or dunny, one of the better situated for the amateur astronomer. On the whole there are more clear nights in the outback than in Britain, not to mention a better view of Halley's comet. I expect the British version has its own night noises – the stifled mutterings of hunt saboteurs, the snuffling of moles – and in the USA the little house on the prairie probably resounds to the grunting of grizzlies and the gentle gurgle of oil wells.

Not that one hears a lot about either of these. The North Americans are notoriously coy about the natural functions and the British tend to find the bidet funnier than the bog. It is in Australia that the Dunny really comes into its own. Just why it should loom so large in the antipodean imagination is curious. My theory is that it is because the wildlife likely to inhabit it is so much more lethal than any in England or North America. The chances of finding a grizzly bear enthroned are probably remote, because of the difficulty such a beast would have in fitting in, whereas deadly snakes and spiders – the Redback on the toilet seat syndrome – have easy access. This may have rendered the Aussie Dunny a source of nightmares likely to imprint permanently on the young mind.

I well remember the nervous shudder I felt when, on holiday in the country as a schoolgirl, I was required to go before bedtime. Not only were there – oh horror – ghastly possibilities lurking in the inky shadows inside the structure itself, but also cobwebs strung across the garden path waiting to clutch at my face as I crept, torch in hand, towards the pit. These were re-hung nightly by determined Orb-spinning spiders, one of the few non-lethal local species, but nevertheless huge, hairy, and unbelievably horrible. The mere thought of one dropping onto the back of my neck as I passed was enough to induce permanent fluid retention.

Since then Australia has become less obsessed with dunnies, most of which have become the victims of modern plumbing, unmourned even by keen industrial archaeologists. Lavatory humour has fallen into disrepute.

It is therefore rather retrograde of me to mention this coarse feature of country life – it was mainly in the country they were to be found – but I feel I must share a couple of stories I picked up recently from my aunt, a fertile source of historical data.

During World War 2 there existed in South Australia an organization called The Children's Patriotic Fund. Its aim was to aid the War Effort by collecting as much newspaper and tinfoil as possible. Children were encouraged to bring their collections to school, and at the end of each week a reward was given to the child who had collected the most. It was the duty of one of my aunt's young nephews to cut the household's old newspapers into neat squares with a hole in one corner, thread them onto a piece of string and hang them on a hook behind the lavatory door. Noticing that the supply was running out his mother reminded him that it was about time he replenished it.

'Blow that!' he replied. 'I'm not going to waste good newspaper in the dunny – I collected more newspapers than any kid in the school last week!'

About the same year, the local doctor's small daughter started school. During her first week her mother noticed that she was coming home every day with soiled knickers.

'Sheila' she said to her gently, 'You really must use paper when you go to the toilet you know.'

'But Mum,' the poor child replied, 'The big girls take all the newspaper. And the big boys take all the smooth stones!'

Think about it when you're the Supermarket trying to decide between the quilted DownySoft and the aloe vera impregnated FeatherTouch.

CHRISTMAS DOWN UNDER

Ah, Christmas! The North wind shall blow, and sunburns will glow, and what will the Aussies do then, poor things?

They'll do what they do every year. They'll send each other Christmas cards depicting carollers in the snow, and English Robins singing on bare boughs. Admittedly there is an increasing traffic in raised consciousness cards showing Santa resting beneath a gum tree – or possibly a Coolibah – with his coat off and a can of Fosters in his hand. But on the whole, snow and holly predominate. And, on The Day, a goodly number will be doing just what I'll be doing myself; steaming the pudding, peeling the spuds and basting the fatted chook in preparation for that annual family festivity, the Christmas Dinner.

In the farm kitchen the old wood stove, stoked to fever pitch to get the potatoes really crisp, will raise the room temperature to forty-six degrees C., so that the forty-one outside – that's a hundred and five on the old scale, as any DJ will tell you – is a welcome relief, to be enjoyed for a blissful moment when the rinse-water from the potatoes is emptied onto the thirsty garden.

My Mother-in-Law, dressed in baggy shorts and vest, and surely losing as much precious fluid per second as the pudding steamer, beats and bastes with stoic fortitude. The pink paper hat clinging damply to her forehead must be driving her mad, but the grandchildren crowned her, so she ignores it.

Every time anyone leaves or enters the house the bloated blowflies clinging to the wire mesh of the screen door zoom in, driven to a frenzy by the aroma of roasting meat, and buzz like loopy dive-bombers in agonies of frustration over the covered dishes. Only the blowflies and the humans, each crazy in their own way, are active. The rest of the world, with sound common sense, conserves its energy. The dog lies panting on the veranda, the cows congregate in the few patches of shade. The horse stands beneath a tree and hangs his head, motionless except for an occasional toss of the head to brush away the small bushflies that crawl around his eyes searching for moisture.

Snakes that spent the morning soaking up the sun retreat into their holes before their blood boils. Even the gum-trees hang down their leaves to avoid the glare.

But inside the house, sons and daughters-in-law push tables together, or dust off the table-tennis table to accommodate the increasing numbers of couples and children, and set out the wedding-present silver and dinner service, placing beside each plate a Christmas cracker decorated with a snowman.

Mother changes her shorts and vest for a cotton dress, and everyone, including the flies, sits down to a hot roast dinner. Die-hard inheritors of a snow-born tradition.

Eventually the pudding is brought in, its brandy flaming. The blinds are already drawn, to keep out the heat. At this stage they are probably keeping just as much in, but the gloom makes it easier to see the spectacle.

There are even proper silver sixpences and threepences in this pudding; saved from the days when we had real money, instead of these newfangled decimal things that poison the mixture.

These are ritually examined, and returned to Grandma (sometimes not without argument) to be washed and hoarded away for next Christmas. Lucky finders are reimbursed at the current rate of exchange, over which there is usually some disagreement.

At last the feast is over, and everyone feels prostrated, torpid, and utterly spent, with an urgent desire to emulate the other animals and sleep. Even the blowflies can only buzz in drunken circles.

However a further effort is called for; the flies cannot be permitted free range of the remains, and the women spend the rest of the afternoon doing dishes, mitigating the dreariness by gossiping. Weddings, adulteries and divorces, pregnancies and miscarriages, ailments and remedies, errant children (other people's) and school-prize-winning offspring (ours), the drought (there's always the drought), and The Royals. The Goings-On of the Windsors, beloved of *New Idea* and *Woman's Day*, are always good for a giggle or an indulgent smile. The men entertain the children, attempt to explain the workings of complicated toys, or search for missing pieces of half-assembled models. Children envy each other's Christmas presents, and wrangle. Everyone, although replete, grazes absent-mindedly from the dishes of nuts and sweets left about, or drinks – at least the drinks are cold, if the fridge is still working.

And often late in the evening, when talk and adults are exhausted, and the youngest child grizzles sleeplessly with prickly heat, and the temperature refuses to drop even though the sun has long been set, someone suggests that next year we should have a cold Christmas dinner.

So far, though, neither my in-laws nor my own family, who are duplicating this ritual six hundred kilometres west, has ever done so.

Sadly, there are rumours of an increasing number of Australians breaking with tradition, and going over to cold collations and ice-cream cake. Salads with sand and sunburn on the beach. An Esky packed with ice-cold stubbies for the grown-ups and soft drinks for the kids. Father Christmas in a wet-suit.

I say sadly because, no matter how patently idiotic a custom may be, if it's part of one's childhood its passing must cause a wrench; and to me, Christmas isn't Christmas even in the bush, without the trappings of my Northern forefathers. Ah, Christmas. Paper snowflakes on schoolroom windows. Good King Wenceslas and frostbite. Jingle Bells, Tiny Tim, plastic holly and canned snow – and above all, a climatically inappropriate, medically deplorable, absolutely wonderful Hot Christmas Dinner.

WORDS AND PHRASES

One of the advantages, for an Australian, of living in London or in Columbus, Ohio, rather than in Moscow or Athens, is that the locals speak English, or almost. Having lived in both London and Columbus I've discovered that it is possible to be lulled into a false sense of security by apparent similarities in vocabulary. It becomes rapidly apparent in Britain that terminology depends to an enormous extent on the class of the speaker, which would be fine if there were a few more obvious indications as to what that class was. The British derive considerable satisfaction and pleasure from classifying each other according to lineage, profession, accent, dress, money, and whether they drink proper coffee or instant. However since no two people seem to agree on any classification and the class of any one person appears to be that which he has decided fits him, poor foreigners get terribly muddled.

Particularly since the people he happens to be with at any time have probably put him into a different class. (Confusion about which class you or, indeed, anybody else belongs to is, I'm told, a reliable indication of Middle-Classness).

If only all working class members wore flat caps, all the bourgeoisie bow ties and all toffs, toppers, it would be a simple matter to decide what each meant by the word 'supper'.

Toppers – crepes Suzette after the Opera. Bow-ties – evening meal with the family. Flat cap – something the Upper class has after the Opera. I've probably got that all round the wrong way because I *still*, after five years here, don't know who means what by 'tea' 'supper' and 'dinner'. At least 'lunch' seems to be universally accepted, though it wouldn't surprise me to discover that in certain sections of society to have lunch at all is still infra dig. (I gleaned that information from Trollope).[1]

For a long time I thought that the reason all the children my own invited home to tea toyed with my pizzas and hamburgers was that they just didn't like my cooking. Or because they recognised only crisps and Mars Bars as food. As I got to know more of the locals I realized that for tea, these children had been expecting a glass of squash and a biscuit at four o'clock, not a two-course meal at six. That was waiting for them at home, and was called either supper or dinner. In our house, when the kids come in after school and stuff themselves with whatever junk food and drink they can find before flinging their weary bodies in front of the television, that's called afternoon tea. On weekends and holidays it happens at about eleven a.m. as well and is called morning tea. 'Tea' is the family evening meal and is eaten at six or, if we can bear to wait that long, whenever Daddy gets home.

'Dinner' is reserved for the sort of meals that cost a week's wages and to which adult friends are invited and children, having been fed hours beforehand, barred on the grounds that they hog the conversation. They may be permitted to hand round nuts and things to the guests while Mummy tears her hair out in the kitchen. Supper, alas, we almost never have. Supper is a snack before bedtime or if you're lucky and rich, after the theatre. Not being rich we spend the interlude after rare evenings out

---

[1] Anthony. I didn't discover Joanna until 1988

running for the last train. Hot chocolate and crumpets went out when the bathroom scales came in.

One of the dangers of getting the terms wrong is that of arriving fully fed at a host's groaning board and having to face another meal knowing that your hostess has slaved all day, and that it is your *duty* to eat and look as though you liked it. This happened to us once in the American midwest, our first experience of supper as the major meal. At least supper *always* meant the evening meal in Ohio so we didn't make the same mistake twice.

The pitfalls of assumed similarity are great in the States, but when you've fallen into one, you know it. An Australian friend once boarded a bus in Columbus and sat next to a young woman struggling to control a wriggling baby and a lapful of parcels.

'May I nurse the baby for you?' he offered.

Everyone within earshot froze, and the woman shrank away in horror. 'Nurse' meant exclusively to breast-feed, not as my Australian meant, to hold.

I once got a similar reaction from a department store waitress when I asked her for a white coffee. (Fortunately she was a white waitress).

'White cawfee?' she said a little nervously. 'What's that?'

Under these surprising circumstances the phrase 'with milk' completely deserted me.

'Er – you know – not black.' I said.

Light dawned. 'Oh, you mean cawfee with *cream*!' she chortled. 'Y'know, we had another Englishman in here earlier. Wanted to know what sort of ice we had. Well, I said, just regular ice – cold and hard! – Turned out he wanted *sherbet*. What part of the Old Country you from?'

With the exception of an ex-GI who'd been on R and R in Sydney in '45 ('Wouldn't happen to know a gal called Sue Brown, would you?') Americans took us for Brits, or occasionally Austrians with amazingly good English. Not mistakes that are ever made in London. Here the reaction is usually a slightly disparaging smile such as one might give an habitual H-dropper, or a positive beam and a detailed account of a trip to visit the grandchildren in Melbourne.

Once a slightly pissed Pom telephoned twice within two minutes to hear me tell him that he had a wrong number, and enunciated my words in a clear parody to giggling friends in the background.

But where the English have developed the insult to a fine art, the Americans have carried the compliment to the point of embarrassment.

'Ah just *lerv* your accent!' was their constant cry. 'Doesn't she have a *darling* accent, honey? Say "I've just joined the A.A.A." again!'

No American could understand any word I pronounced with an 'A' in it – I was once asked to describe an 'ipple' because the person I was talking to had never heard of one. 'One of those fruits you make pies with.' I said. 'Starts with the first letter of the alphabet.'

When I applied for laboratory jobs to supplement my student husband's scholarship I was consistently directed to the Ladies Lavatory for the interview until I learned to shorten it to 'lab'. I couldn't handle '*lab*-ra-tory' without stumbling. Hospital staff always directed me to the Lavatory with some embarrassment, since this is a somewhat crude term for what is politely referred to as the bathroom, the John, the Little Girls Room, the powder room, or even, I noticed in one restaurant, Squaws and Braves.

On the whole there don't seem to *be* many uniquely Australian words. Which seems a bit of a pity really. They might give us a bit of national character. It is sometimes tiresome to he seen as either an inferior Englishwoman or an inferior American. Of course there is Billabong and Bowyang and Boomerang, and the famous Barcoo salute. And Kangaroo and Koala and Kookaburra. But somehow nouns don't seem to count.

What we need are a few good descriptive words and phrases. The Aussie equivalent of 'Swan-Upping' or 'losing your rag'. Of course we don't actually Up Swans, but perhaps 'emu-necking' might catch on as an annual ritual. And possibly 'losing your swag?'

Due to my genteel education in a state that prides itself on its non-convict origins, I may have overlooked some Eastern States ockerisms[1], but a quick trawl through the memory has produced only two descriptives which *may* be unique – 'crook' meaning poorly – *that's* a very British word, by the way – and 'snaky', meaning venomous or bitchy as in 'She's a snaky piece, that one!' It doesn't seem a lot for two hundred years.

Still, things are probably better as they are. International Understanding is probably preferable to National Character, anyway.

---

[1] Ocker: An archetypal Australian working man, vulgar, unsophisticated, boorish.

WEATHER

It was sleeting when we arrived back in London. Oh, to be in England, now that April's here. Though to be honest, it had been decidedly chilly in Victoria, four days earlier. We'd had wood fires at night, and the cow's breath hung foggily on the morning air, for those up with the galah to see. I skulked in bed with a long flannel nightie covering my fast-fading suntan. The tan came from Perth. That's Perth, Western Australia, where it had been thirty-five degrees centigrade at midnight when we arrived, all unprotected in our tender British skins.

Life in a hot climate has its drawbacks. Within a week the children's skins had sloughed off in dirty brown strips, accompanied by frenzied itching preceded by three days of agonizing sunburn. The sunburn was complicated in one case by an allergy to almost every brand of sunburn lotion, of which there were an amazing number, at mind-boggling prices. By the third day I was the only member of the family capable of making the long, hot trek to the chemists. The others were either spreadeagled semi-naked on the bed with a headache, or drooping in cane chairs in the air-conditioned hotel lobby, with scarcely enough energy to press the buttons on the pocket computer games they'd bought at the Duty Free.

It was my fault, of course. I should have remembered that deadly UV rays bounce off the surface of the swimming pool. We were all seduced by the jewel-like water, so deliciously cool, the palms and frangipani and the little white, umbrella shaded tables, where smiling waitresses served ice-cold stubbies of Emu Export Lager. The pool, of course, was not shaded, but I failed to notice that at the time. Swimming pools and tropical vegetation are my abiding memories of Perth.

The tropical aspect surprised me. I'd always thought of Perth as an extension of the Nullarbor Plain, a sort of Australian Sahara. This view is not entirely in error. Beyond the suburban environs of Perth much of it does seem like that. But Perth is much closer to the tropic of Capricorn than I'd realised, and sits atop an apparently endless supply of underground water. With water, and a hefty helping of sheep dung to hold the sand together, bougainvillea, hibiscus, staghorn ferns and other lush and fragrant flora flourish. The water that supports them is not so fragrant. At certain hours of the morning and evening the atmosphere around Bull Creek – Perth's answer to Beverley Hills[1] – has a distinctly sulphurous pong. Foreigners from Melbourne wrinkle their noses and mutter about the drains.

The sulphur doesn't seem to do the plants any harm, but it does leave grubby yellow watermarks on the walls and footpaths, so that it is possible to tell even in dry hours, which properties have their own bores. Which seems to be practically all of them. Cunningly sunk among the shrubs and lawns – most of which stretch unbroken to the roadside – a score of sprinklers await the computers command, and at a pre-set signal leap into odorous life with a mighty SKSHHH! drenching the unsuspecting passer-by. The water in the swimming pools, of which there are also a goodly number, simply smells of chlorine.

Pool owners are extremely disgruntled at a recent Federal Government tax on pool chemicals and equipment. They say it will discourage owners from sterilizing the water regularly and

---

[1] Apolgies to residents of Dalkieth and Applecross, which I'm told are perhaps more Beverley Hills. Frankly, after South London, the whole of Perth seemed like Beverley Hills.

make it a health hazard. Even sunburn lotion is subject to luxury tax, curious considering the many public warnings against skin cancer. If this situation continues, Perthites may be reduced to adopting Arab dress, and cooling off under their garden sprinklers.

The city had experienced a month of temperatures over forty degrees when we arrived. (That's a hundred and four Fahrenheit to you). Those who speak of the sun *beating* down know what they're talking about. It hits the top of the head like a hammer blow. You'd think that under those conditions anything that breathed would stay indoors (even the flies were conspicuously absent) but not so. Probably their numbers were severely depleted – being a visitor I couldn't tell – but there were still plenty of bodies clad in nothing but bikinis disporting themselves on the beach at Canning River. I'll swear you could have cooked an egg on some of those glowing backs.

The compulsion to rush to the nearest water whenever the sun shines overrode even the survival instinct. Instead of sensibly donning a shady hat, choosing a patch of water and sitting in it up to the neck till sundown, they were cavorting about on sailboards, diving off bridges, and indulging in the innocent antipodean pastime of jellyfish hurling. These were not lethal Portugese-men-o'war, but two meeker varieties, one a pale beige umbrella, the other a saucer of delicate translucent blue. Ranging in size from fingertip to dinner plate, their gently pulsating bodies fill Perth's tidal rivers in thousands in the summer. With so many submissive missiles to hand, the bathers obviously felt that it was a pity not to throw one at somebody.

When we transferred ourselves from the hotel to a friend's house our sympathetic hostess took us to the Canning River in an effort to take the children's minds off their peeling backs. She drove us there in her blissfully air-conditioned car, which she left coyly hiding its face behind fan-shaped Venetian blinds to shade the interior, while we sat under a tree eating ice creams and observing the antics of the suicidal pleasure-seekers.

It was one of the few forays we made out of doors during our entire stay in Perth, and only a combination of threats and bribery succeeded in getting one child to come at all. When I announced brightly, 'Marilyn's taking us to Deep Point,' he flung himself to his knees beside a lounge, buried his face in the cushions and growled: 'Don't *want* to go to Deep Point. Don't want to go *anywhere*. I want to go back to England!'

And so, after a couple of months had elapsed during which Australia cooled down and England warmed up (though not much), we did.

Though not before we'd had a few adventures – but that's another story.

SATURDAY NIGHT AT THE MOVIES

We were cruising down Perth's Swan River when I saw, with a sudden pang of nostalgia, a reminder of my childhood. It rose above the plain like a cricket sightscreen for giants.
'What's that, Mum?' asked the children.
'That,' I said, 'Is a Drive-in Theatre Screen.'
I was about ten when drive-in movies arrived in Australia. They seemed to spring up on every vacant block. Everybody went. Summer Saturday nights in the car, parents in front, kids in the back with pillows and a rug for when the youngest fell asleep. Courting couples with their heads together. Even an occasional cyclist with a folding canvas chair, confident of remaining warm and dry, because most of Australia possesses the essential elements for outdoor cinema – long, dry, summers, without twilight. The sun sets earlier, but once it's gone, it's gone. It doesn't hover uncertainly on the horizon trying to make up its mind, but, sinking into the sea with an almost audible hiss, leaves behind an inky blackness; the perfect background for displaying *South Pacific*. They showed family films then – the sort that could be accused neither of education nor corruption, but left the audience feeling cheerful enough to face another night of simmering temperatures.
In our country town the drive-in was erected in the paddock next to the Australian Broadcasting Corporation

transmitter station where my father worked, and for a while there was some confusion between the film sound track and the local radio programme, due to underground cables being too close together. Eventually it was sorted out but, until then, Dad could, while on night shift, watch the current movie, with soundtrack, through the window.

They weren't 'movies' in those days, though, they were 'the pictures' or, if you happened to be a Queenslander, 'the fillums'. The venue, even if it was a drive-in, was a 'theatre'. The 'cinema' was where the English went.

The drive-in consisted of a vast field, divided into semi-circular rows of little humps, beside each of which stood a metal pole housing a speaker. About halfway down the field stood a double-storeyed concrete building with projecting room above, and snack bar below. Everything was angled towards the screen, a towering edifice on metal legs. The whole was usually surrounded on at least three sides by a high corrugated iron fence, to discourage freeloaders.

In order to watch in maximum comfort, one arrived early – preferably before sunset – and chose a spot about mid-field, not too far from the screen, but not so close that the car was angled so steeply that everyone got a crick in the neck. Next one checked that the speaker worked – that the volume could be adjusted both up *and* down – and that a previous patron had not irreparably crushed the hook designed to attach it to the car window. Someone then went for a supply of sweets and drinks.

Meanwhile a queue of vehicles formed up along the road, and crawled slowly past the ticket office, where the salesperson kept an eye skinned for backseat stowaways secreted under rugs. Gradually the ground filled up, the front wheels of each car resting on its carefully angled hump. Late arrivals forced into the front rows found themselves almost lying on their backs, and drinking or eating became positively foolhardy. It soon became an inflexible family rule that all drinking took place *outside* the vehicle.

Windows were wound down to admit the breeze, and as darkness fell, heated arguments arose about who was to sit where and for how long. (Parents usually got the front seat during the second feature – there *was* a second feature before blockbusters – while small children dozed in the back, though this arrangement necessitated the parents sitting atop a litter of spilt popcorn).

As the first Technicolor giants flickered across the screen, the mosquitoes arrived, and a battle ensued between those who wanted the windows *up*, to keep the insects out, and those who wanted them *down* to let the cool air in. The latter always won, because closing *all* the windows completely meant removing the speaker, thus making the movie silent. The inevitable outcome never prevented the argument, though.

By autumn the mozzies became less of a problem, but there was usually at least one chilly body who closed every possible aperture so that our breath fogged up the windscreen.

As winter approached audiences thinned, though a few courting couples remained giving an occasional glance at the screen through a peephole wiped in the steamy glass.

But come summer, Disney and Rank would pack them in again.

When we left for the UK in 1980 they were still there, the Drive-in Theatres, in spite of television, but patronised mostly by knowing teenagers watching the sort of movie that parents prefer not to know about. Family entertainment had been relegated to the small screen. I doubted that the Drive-In would survive the video. I supposed the screens would be melted down for scrap, which would at least remove a few eyesores from the landscape.[1]

---

[1] In 2008 the drive-in was alive and well in Australia, though many went bust in the 80's. Those that remained have prospered and some now even have three screens and an outdoor seating area for walkers and cyclists.

But it did seem a pity. You don't have the same sense of *occasion*, sitting in front of the television.

JET TRAILS IN THE SUNSET

Though I hope I am a woman of peace, there are one or two people I could cheerfully help into the infinite, and one of them is the passenger who, on a recent flight, refused to extinguish his cigarette on takeoff and landing. He insisted that he needed it for his nerves. This confirms my view that the most dangerous, as well as the most irritating, things on an aeroplane are the other passengers. Quite apart from the risk of all 400 passengers having their neuroses permanently cured by one such lunatic, a more lingering end may be in store for those of us forced to inhale the carcinogens wafting over us from the smoking section in front. There is an unwritten law that the chain-smokers will always be seated in the last row of the smoking section, where they can cause maximum discomfort to those behind. I know, because on all but one of the seven legs of our journey to, from, and around Australia my family and I were sitting behind them.

As the 'No Smoking' lights go out for the first time, the voice of the captain is heard announcing that smoking is now permitted – 'but please, for the comfort of other passengers, no pipes or cigars.' Comfort my foot – it's because pipes and cigars can't be extinguished as efficiently as cigarettes, and a smouldering briar in someone's pocket might –

well, use your imagination.[1] Or so my husband told me somebody else had told *him*, though he may have been making it all up, since I notice that a certain European airline does allow pipes and cigars 'provided there is no complaint from any other passenger.' I have not investigated their safety record, but I intend to give them a wide berth.[2]

Not only do other passengers smoke, snore, and recline their seats with sudden ferocity, precipitating coffee into one's lap; they also make up (and possibly out, but that's their own business).

At 4 a.m. on the midnight flight from Perth to Melbourne (they call it the Redeye Special) just as the captain had switched on all the cabin lights yet *again*, under the completely erroneous impression that I wished to know that we were flying at 29,000 feet and the weather in Melbourne was cool, some unspeakable female across the aisle opened her make-up case and gave herself a complete facial. She used half a dozen highly scented beauty aids, finishing off with a dab of perfume behind the ears. The effect in the enclosed atmosphere resembled that of being locked in a telephone booth with somebody soaked in a mixture of paraffin and Chanel. Short of shoving one of those little airline pillows – they must be useful for something – over her face the instant she reaches for the lipstick, I doubt whether much can be done about this abomination. Males are not guiltless, either. And I don't care if his aftershave *did* cost a bomb, in combination with aviation fuel and bacon and eggs it smells revolting. It's enough to put a person off her roll and marmalade.

Airline food is much maligned. It is not the food that's plastic, but those horrid containers that fly off the tray at

---

[1] Written c.1985. Kathy Reich's 2001 novel *Fatal Voyage* involves this scenario.
[2] Since about 1998 almost, but not quite, all airlines have banned smoking for passengers.

the touch of a fork. Some of the stuff we had was quite good, and travelling as a family had the advantage that individual cheeses could always be traded for somebody else's chocolate biscuits. Anyway, as everyone knows, the purpose of airline food is not to sustain the body but to occupy the mind. An international flight is like a stay in hospital; a long sentence punctuated by meals. There you are, confined in a small uncomfortable space under a benevolent dictatorship, most of the time bored rigid and always with an underlying sense of unease at the possibility that you may not get out alive. Meals become little landmarks to which, unless feeling positively ill, you look forward with a kind of desperation – only three to go till L.A., or if they're calling this breakfast we must be almost at Bombay.

According to the glossy airline magazine, airsickness does not exist any more, though for our comfort a waterproof paper bag has been placed in the front seat pocket. This is the equivalent of the Dentist's assurance that it won't hurt a bit. Unfortunately one airline we flew with took its own propaganda seriously and failed to provide the bag. The magazine also soothingly stated that pain in the ears is now a thing of the past with modern pressurised aircraft; a slight discomfort that would disappear once cruising altitude was reached being all we would feel. Naturally, take-off and landing resulted in one child clutching its head between its knees, its keening wail audible above the roar of the engines, and the other hunched, chalk-white, over a sick-bag, retching and gasping. The sick-bag was grudgingly provided from stores once it was apparent that we meant business, with the withering 'You're only doing this to annoy me' look perfected by all nurses.

It took me a few take-offs to realise that the glass of free bubbly I accepted once we'd broken the pain barrier gave me a thumping headache. The cabin crew then put into effect the 'No eye-contact with demanding passengers' ploy, otherwise known as 'Nobody gets any aspirin until we've finished serving the dinners.' This tactic was also employed during the actual serving of the meal, which they placed before all alike, including the parchment-faced nine-year old with the sick-bag and the lucky one fast sleep. My meek protests were ignored in their swift passage on to the next row of patients, and I was left to juggle three trays of unwanted food until clearing-up time, because one child refused to have food near it and the other woke up and wanted to use the table to hold a book.

The other airline – the one that *did* have little bags already in the seat pocket – also provided a puzzle book and coloured pencils for the children. A continuous soundtrack on one of the entertainment channels – we were all given earphones, which gave half the passengers the appearance of doctors solemnly using their stethoscopes – gave instructions about the puzzles and an amusing commentary that kept my son occupied, with breaks for sleep and regurgitation, all the way from Melbourne to L.A.

Airport bookshops give the impression that reading is a major pastime on an aircraft. They lure the unsuspecting traveller with doorstop-sized tomes encrusted with gold lettering and cover blurbs promising enough sex, intrigue, or rambling royalist romance to cocoon the most fearful flier. How can anything bad happen when one is in Rutshire with Rupert-Campbell-Black, or sipping cocktails in a casino with a re-issued James Bond? Certainly not a sudden drop from 35,000 feet.

It's all a con. Reading on a plane is almost an anti-social activity, because it interferes with the In-Flight Movie. At least half an hour before the movie begins, the crew pull down all the blinds, plunging the cabin into darkness. Should a passenger be seized with the insane desire to take a peek at the passing clouds, one of the crew will politely lower her blind, explaining that the sunlight will make it difficult for others to see the movie. This, of course, means that should you want to read you must use your personal light, which, should you be sitting directly in line with the screen, will also cause interference. Few travellers are tough enough to rebel against the tyranny of the In-Flight Movie. They wait for the two to three hours it takes to run, by which time the plane has usually flown into the dark, and read during the short time it might be possible for others to sleep, if their peripheral vision wasn't dazzled by some inconsiderate insomniac's reading light. To be fair, there are some points – though not many – in favour of the I.F.M. By tuning your headset to the channel reserved for the forward cabin, you can desynchronise the sound and action, giving female actors men's voices and vice versa, and having periods of silence during which they open and close their mouths like goldfish. Or you might have the soundtrack of a completely different movie. It adds a new dimension. Or the movie may constantly break down, which can be quite enjoyable. The James Bond we saw between London and Bombay broke down so often (and always in the most exciting parts) that the little boy in front finally declared in disgust, 'This is a *stupid* telly!'

Which reminds me that I heard a dreadful rumour recently. It has been suggested that video screens be put into planes so that passengers, who might otherwise suffer severe withdrawal symptoms, can see the latest television news. Personally, the last thing I want to hear when I'm seven miles up and it's minus 38 outside, is that another 747 has just flown into the side of an Exocet. Nor do I particularly care to be informed about wars, famines, or Acts of God in any of the countries I am flying to or from. Or even over. I believe, though, that the word 'edited' may have been used in connection with this service. What, I wonder, could they leave *in*? The Royal Engagements?

Oh, for the days when people travelled by ship. A bottle of seasick pills, a good book and a place to hide, is all I ask. And yet, when my feet are firmly on the ground, I can't help feeling nostalgic about flying. Like Londoners and the Blitz. They know it was awful, but they can't help feeling that somehow, in some way, there was something good about it. So when I'm in the garden of a summer evening and I see those jet trails in the sunset, I still feel a flutter of envy for the passengers bound for far away places with strange-sounding names.

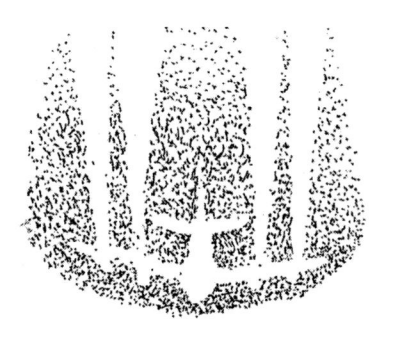

Mayday, Mayday

Hooray, hooray, they've gone, they've *gone*. And they've gone without tears, without fuss, without the usual tantrums and traumas and 'I *won't* wear green knickers!' and 'I *won't* eat wholemeal bread sandwiches!'

Could it be that they've finally realised my threats to leave home were serious?

Did my daughter realise the significance of the library book I chose for her holiday reading? (It's about divorce and the heroine a twelve-year old girl. Mine's nine, but bright for her age. Too lazy to walk to the library and choose her own books, though).

It's a marvellous read (well I enjoyed it) by Judy Bloome, entitled *It's not the end of the world*. One of the early indications that all is not hunky-dory between Mom and Dad occurs when Mom hurls a newly-baked mocha fudge chocolate cake to the floor, a scene so hideously close to our family bone that that my daughter can't have failed to make the connection.

Mind you, things would have to be *really* bad at our house before I'd destroy a perfectly good chocolate cake like that. The plate, yes. The cake, never. In that situation I'd have been down there on the floor with the heroine, salvaging the china-free bits, as soon as the rest of the family had cleared off.

I might have been able to bring myself to fling food of another colour though – a trifle, say, or spaghetti Bolognese. I've been tempted more than once to upend the latter over somebody's head.

It's chocolate I couldn't bear to dispose of – except by eating it. In fact it may have been this that made the children finally realise how close I was to cracking. They drove me to chocolate. They drove me to drink, too. And cigarettes.

We always have plenty of duty-free whisky given to us by overseas visitors, so supply was no problem. The trouble was that while it dulled the pain to some extent, it made me so sleepy that in the end I became even crabbier, because who can sleep surrounded by howling demons? What I needed was something to calm my nerves without rendering me incapable of movement.

I tried sucking my thumb, but it doesn't taste as good as it did when I was six. So I bought some cigarettes. Of course I couldn't set the children a bad example, so I hid in the vegetable garden.

I knew they'd never find me there – they wouldn't risk being asked to pull up a weed. I might never have been found out had my husband not discovered the packet of matches that fell out of my back pocket as I hunkered down behind the raspberries, *willing* the nicotine into my bloodstream, and telling myself it was better to feel sick than suicidal.

But in the end, battered by sibling rivalry and bruised by childish barbarity, I could no longer resist the one comfort left to me. I went and bought myself a box of chocolates, and *ate the lot*. Well all but four. My daughter caught me creeping upstairs with them and recognised the box instantly. Probably from a television commercial. Boxes of chocolate are as rare in our house as offers to wash the dishes.

'Ooh, yummy!' She cried.

'Back!'' I snarled, clutching them to my chest. 'These are *mine*!'

And I continued callously on. But halfway up I was overcome by guilt – how could *I* have borne a similar denial? And I whipped back downstairs and dragged her into the under-stairs cupboard, out of sight of the three boys shooting guns and leaping on my front-room furniture.

'Alright,' I muttered. 'You can have four. And you are *not* to pick them over; you are to take the first four that come to hand and if you tell the boys I will wring your cotton-pickin' neck! O.K.?'

She gazed at me with wild surmise, took some, and slunk away. I think that's when she realised I'd been pushed too far.

Not that there was an instant improvement in behaviour. Certainly not from her brother, who probably considers maternal deprivation a way of life, and not something any change in his own behaviour is likely to alter. Over the years we have achieved a balance – he is deprived of an endless supply of crisps, six hours of television daily and a complete set of weapons capable of destroying man and alien, and I am deprived of sleep and sanity.

It was necessary to face them with the possibility of permanent deprivation of *me* to achieve a minimum of civilised behaviour.

His sister, who is almost two years his senior, had read about boarding schools as well as about divorce, and I suspect she had a quiet word – no, that's hardly possible – a lot of loud words – about the alternative to a rabid, but present, mother. About the possibility of confinement in institutions where nasty bullies steal your teddy-bear, and you have to eat lumpy porridge and greens under the gimlet-eyed gaze of masters who creep about flicking canes and chuckling evilly to themselves.

The reason I didn't hear this harangue (and I'm pretty sure there was one) is that by the end of the school holidays I'd taken more or less permanent refuge in the vegetable garden, where I spent many a peaceful hour picking over windfalls and pulling weeds, with the sound of battle a mere drone in the distance.

It's very therapeutic, weeding. Particularly if you let the weeds grow to a decent height, as I do. After all, they have as much right to life as the rest of us. My policy is to let as many as possible reach maturity, flower, and spread their seed about before I execute them. This has manifold advantages. A good stand of willowherb grows almost as tall as me, and when after a mighty struggle I've rooted it out, I can *see* that I've achieved something. I have that sense of satisfaction at a job well done, the moral glow (akin to eating a free-range hen) of having done right by the plant, and the knowledge that next year, when the summer holidays are again upon us, there will be another forest of weeds ready to sublimate my desire to wring the necks of my offspring.

In the meantime they have at last gone to school, only faintly grumbling, with clean shoes and handkerchiefs, and I can contemplate six hours of peace without the need for a fix of chocolate.

Though if you'd care to donate, there *is* half-term coming up soon – and of course there's Christmas. I prefer the dark sort. With nuts.

BUSY DOING NOTHING

I recently discovered that I am a member of a minority. According to a newspaper article published not long ago, there are not many of us in Britain. Housewives, that is. Those who don't go out to work for wages.

Have you ever noticed, by the way, how percentages seem to have more to do with adjectives than with numbers? If it is reported that 'an alarming one percent' of the population suffers from scurvy, you immediately discover several cases among your friends and start looking for tell-tale signs in yourself; similarly if 'a mere ten percent of school leavers' get to University, you despair of your own child's chances. (In case you're worried, I made those figures up on the spur of the moment. But you see what I mean).

So when I read that 'only' fifteen percent of women in Britain were full-time housewives we suddenly became as scarce as parking places in Oxford Street.

Then I read an article by one of the Few, one well qualified to do otherwise if she chose – she had a degree in Higher Physics or Macro-economics, or something – describing the value of her life as Career Wife and Mother. And more power to her Hoover. But I was not comforted.

It's not that I think there's anything shameful about being a housewife. Only about being a bad one. Like me. Once, I thought that I could merge with the crowd. Now that I know I'm one of a minority I feel exposed, like someone in an orchestra playing a wrong note in one of the quiet bits. Someone will notice that not only do I not contribute to the economy, my floors don't shine either. And the *really* shameful confession is that while I don't particularly want to be a housewife, neither do I want to work.

You see, I've tried it, and found it wanting. Well, to be honest, it was I who was found wanting. It wasn't just one job I was no good at, but several. I was no good at any of them, though I stayed in some longer than others. I've been a housewife for thirteen years now – the longest I've ever been in one position. Mind you, there's not a lot of promotion in it, but then I'm used to that. I never got beyond 'Junior' at anything else either.

I expect that I haven't been sacked yet because the management's a bit lax, quite frankly. It's probably the worker participation that does it. I must say it's a real perk to be able to warm my frozen feet on the Boss's back, even if the hours aren't very conjugal. I mean congenial.

His only stipulation on giving me the job was that he should have two clean shirts a day to choose from, ironed, and with all buttons intact. It wasn't a lot to ask, but even there I've failed. Several times he's had to go to work unironed, and even unbuttoned. (He would have done it himself, but he'd have missed his train). Secretaries pity him, and colleagues can tell that his wife isn't up to scratch.

It's not that I'm without ambition. In my youth I yearned to emulate Anna Pavlova, Joan Sutherland, and/or Ernest Hemingway. The fact that I grew up to *look* rather like Joan Sutherland more or less ruled out Pavlova; and since I couldn't sing only Hemingway remained. His passport to literary success seemed to be a multiplicity of jobs that furnished writing material. But all my jobs just paid the rent. Many of them didn't even do that, and if I hadn't been living at home with my parents or, later, husband (see above) I probably would have been sleeping rough.

Having failed to gain a scholarship to University, thereby ensuring that I would never discover the structure of DNA,[1] I left school to become a junior laboratory assistant. This was relatively easy, so my basic ineptitude passed almost unnoticed (apart from a couple of incidents I'd really rather not talk about), only really coming to the fore when I began nursing training a few years later.

Patients trembled before my injection tray; and so did I, as I plunged the needle into their innocent buttocks and prayed that I wouldn't cripple them for life. I spilt porridge down the chests of old ladies, and put flowers at the bedsides of hay-fever sufferers. People I'd shaved for surgery were sent back half asleep to be re-done because of the stubble I'd left behind. My bandages unravelled, and toddlers whose urine I was collecting for testing stepped in their potties when my back was turned. Under my guidance bed-screens careered out of control like supermarket trolleys and crashed into the beds of patients in plaster casts. Once, I presented a breakfast of bacon and eggs to a Muslim. After six months, I left for the good of humanity.

Fortunately my father was much more successful at holding down a full-time job than I was, so the parental home was still available as a bolt-hole. Employers were not lining up. I took a job selling carpet-shampooers on commission, door-to-door. Each salesperson was assigned his or her own geographical area, which we worked for a week or two before being relocated. Trundling my machine and shampoo bottle I trudged the leafy foothills suburbs, routinely refused entry to Colonial mansions protected by high padlocked gates. Having failed to penetrate the homes of Adelaide's Old Families I was next assigned an area inhabited by ancients eking out pensions

---

[1] Yes, I know it was discovered when I was seven. You're being picky again.

in the houses they had probably lived in since the 1920s, still with the original linoleum on all floors except, in a few cases, the small living-room. This was quite jolly, as they all welcomed me in, plied me with cups of tea and were quite amenable to a demonstration, though in most cases they regretfully declined to buy. Eventually one with no carpet at all offered to buy a machine and, interpreting this as an act of charity and deeply ashamed at taking money from a pensioner for something she patently didn't need, I persuaded her, with some difficulty, not to buy it. Then I admitted defeat and handed in my shampooer.

My next job was even briefer. This was in a factory making rubber gloves and plastic-coated metal. I was just about capable of doing the first task I was set – pulling racks of fuming rubber gloves out of an oven, peeling them from their moulds and setting them on wire mats to cool. Large numbers somehow stuck together and had to be discarded, and I was painfully slow; but I might have improved, had not someone in the office discovered that I had higher academic qualifications than any other employee. I was promoted to a position where I could be *really* incompetent, handling invoices in the metal-coating department.

Protests that high school chemistry did not qualify me for forms in triplicate were taken for false modesty; and within days plastic coated garden furniture and electricians' buzz bars, usually in the wrong colours, were being delivered to people who had never ordered them. After two months I simply didn't go back again.

Eventually I found a niche in a genetics laboratory, feeding, breeding, and from time to time counting, small flying insects. I spent five happy years at this, only displaying my genius for disorganisation when I came into contact with people. On one University Open Day I produced an incubator full of cooked eggs, instead of the live chick embryos they would have been if I had read the thermostat correctly, and more than one practical class had to be completely altered because I produced forty-thousand fruit flies a week later than they were wanted.

One of the biology tutors finally married me – probably to prevent further disruption in his classes – and took me to America, where I worked in another hospital lab. Although I never managed to achieve a good silver nitrate stain, I was tolerated for my charming personality. Anyway, since it was a morbid pathology lab and the patients were already dead, I couldn't do a lot of harm.

Then I had two babies. At last I had discovered a talent. These peasant hips were just made for reproduction. Unfortunately, actually giving birth is not highly prized these days. It's the bringing up afterwards that counts – and for that Dr. Spock[1] wouldn't award me any prizes. Glenn Doman could use me as an example of how *not* to bring up brighter children.

They're both at school now, so I could go back to work part-time, if I could persuade someone to employ me. Buy a freezer. A second pair of jeans even. It *is* tempting. But not tempting enough. So don't call me and I won't call you.

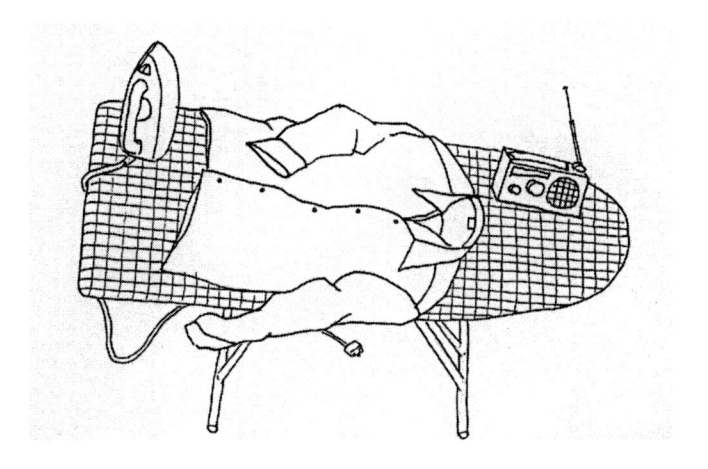

---

[1] Either of them.

NOZTALGIA

Homesickness is something I suffer intermittently. I don't have the crippling variety that makes some people quite literally sick. Mine is more a form of wistful nostalgia. I think I'm past-sick more than homesick really. The symptoms tend to come on when my children are behaving particularly badly, and life is generally miserable. At such times a colour-slide clicks onto the screen of my mind, showing a younger me sitting by the river Murray, in the sun. At my feet the river spreads a wide sheet, dimpled with eddies, to the opposite bank of sheer yellow sandstone cliffs. Above them arches a sky of dazzling blue, and I'm absolutely alone there, somewhere between Renmark and Berri, in the South Australian Riverland.

Well, I haven't sat there like that for years. It's the past I'm hankering for as much as the place: me, free.

Sometimes visions of home will arise quite unbidden and unexpected, usually of places that would be totally uninteresting to a tourist and even to me if I were actually there. I think part of my brain must lead a life of it's own; and it's more homesick than the rest of me. I was reading a biography of William Morris when a picture arose before me – superimposed, as it were, on the one I had of Morris – of a pottery on the Princes Highway in Victoria, displaying earthenware plant pots outside. I've passed this place sometimes while driving, but it has no sentimental associations whatever and no connection I can see with William Morris.

While ironing, shopping, washing dishes or cleaning my teeth I'll be transported to the Adelaide Botanic Gardens, or to a butcher's shop I once patronised, or to a railway station in the Adelaide Hills.

Is this the first sign of softening of the brain? Am I going senile at an unusually early age? Or is my subconscious trying to tell me something? It always seems to be urging me back to the last place I lived in. That's the great disadvantage of moving. It isn't the fields ahead that are greenest; it's the ones behind.

There are things I sometimes long for with a purely present longing, though. For the sight and smell of gum trees, the taste of Vegemite (Marmite is no substitute), ice cream that *isn't* made with non-milk products, the warbling of Australian magpies in the morning.[1] I want to see red deserts and distant purple hills, and endless white beaches with no deck chairs: and a sky full of stars instead of the orange glow of streetlights. And most of all I want some elbowroom.

But then I remember Horse chestnut trees; and I husband the last dregs of the jar of Vegemite left by our recent Aussie visitor; and remind myself that ice cream is bad for your health anyway. And that the blackbirds in our garden sing almost as sweetly as magpies and they don't dive-bomb you if you inadvertently approach their nests.

The desert is very beautiful but incredibly uncomfortable, and while you can't sift beach pebbles between your toes, at least they don't infiltrate your cheese and salad sandwiches. And all the overpoweringly numerous Londoners are on the Tube or in Oxford Street, and it's possible to avoid those most of the time.

Often it isn't the differences about places that affect me as much as the similarities. The South London primary school my children go to is nothing like their little school

---

[1] Vegemite is now widely available in the U.K., as is proper ice-cream.

in South Australia with its staff of two, twenty-eight pupils, and yard planted with grass and gums. But it's very like the school I went to thirty years ago in Adelaide. The uniform is even in the same colours; and most of the four hundred pupils have permanently scarred knees from falling over in the hard playground. There were no school dinners at my school (we ate our packed lunches outside in a corrugated iron shelter shed) nor did I ever see the playground covered with snow. Nevertheless, similarities are so strong that the mere whiff of a London school loo can transport me back twelve thousand miles and thirty years.

When I was very small, Adelaide had London buses – red, double-decker ones. To ride at the front of the top deck and watch the bus apparently swallowing up the people crossing in front of it was one of my delights. But Adelaide's double-deckers vanished years ago. London is full of Time Machines.

Living here is like re-living my past. I doubt whether a Londoner migrating to Adelaide could do the same. Perhaps that's why some British migrants flee from Australia. They say we have no history but I suspect it is reminders of the past in their own lives that they miss. Of course the heat and the flies and the lager, and the terrible disappointment of discovering that there are strikes and unemployment and that it is sometimes actually cold and even rains occasionally, may have something to do with it.

Meantime there are enough reminders of my own past here to make life tolerable, and enough differences to make it interesting – so I think I'll stay.

Notes

Note on notes: You'll have to take my word for it. I'm not going to cite sources. Think yourself lucky to have notes at all! You know how to Google, don't you? And if you don't, you probably remember all this stuff anyway.